BUCKTON CASTLE
and the Castles of North West England

Brian Grimsditch
Michael Nevell &
Richard Nevell

University of Salford
MANCHESTER

© University of Salford and the authors

2012

paperback ISBN 978-0-9565947-2-3
e-book ISBN 978-0-9565947-3-0

University of Salford Archaeological Monographs Volume 2
&
The Archaeology of Tameside Volume 9

First published by the Centre for Applied Archaeology, School of the Built Environment, University of Salford

Design and Artwork by the Centre for Applied Archaeology

Printed by Acorn Print Media, Loughborough
with a grant from the University of Salford Alumni Fund

Contents

Chapter 1
Power, Status and War: The Archaeology of
the Castle in North West England — **Page 1**

Chapter 2
The Political and Social Context of Buckton — **Page 35**

Chapter 3
Excavation and Survey at Buckton Castle — **Page 57**

Chapter 4
Buckton after the Castle — **Page 87**

Chapter 5
A Gazetteer of North West Castles — **Page 99**

Notes — **Page 116**

Sources — **Page 126**

Glossary of Terms — **Page 134**

Acknowledgements — **Page 135**

Index — **Page 136**

Power, Status and War: The Archaeology of the North West Castle CHAPTER 1

Fig 1: Chester Castle, showing the later medieval curtain wall standing on top of the motte erected in 1070 on King William's orders.

Chapter 1

Power, Status and War: The Archaeology of the Castle in North West England

Introduction

In January 1360 a jury of tenants was summoned from across the Lordship of Longdendale; the historic pan-handle of Cheshire. They were tasked to give evidence under oath about landholdings and land values within the upland lordship. The evidence was given in front of officers appointed on behalf of the Black Prince, then earl of Chester and Lord of Longdendale. Amongst the records of that day was a reference to 'one ruined castle called Buckeden and of no value.'[1] This was the first, indeed the only, reference to the enigmatic earthwork at Buckton during this period; it does not tell us who built the castle, nor why. Nor does it explain how the castle fell into ruin.

In later years Buckton was marked on a 16th century estate map, recorded in 18th century estate letters, and from the mid-19th century was the subject of local antiquarian and archaeological curiosity. Interest in the castle was revived during the 1990s and the recent excavations at this site are the culmination of nearly 20 years of archaeological research. The castle is a ruin well known in its immediate locality, although until recently it was largely overlooked as a medieval fortification. This chapter will attempt to place the stone enclosure castle at Buckton within a wider landscape setting that will look at the military, political and social context of the castle in North West England (Fig 1).

The Research and Excavation of Castles in the North West

The term 'castle' covers a wide variety of medieval fortifications and typically refers to a building that is "the fortified residence of a lord", according to Allen Brown.[2] The first castles in England were built by

'one ruined castle called Buckeden and of no value'

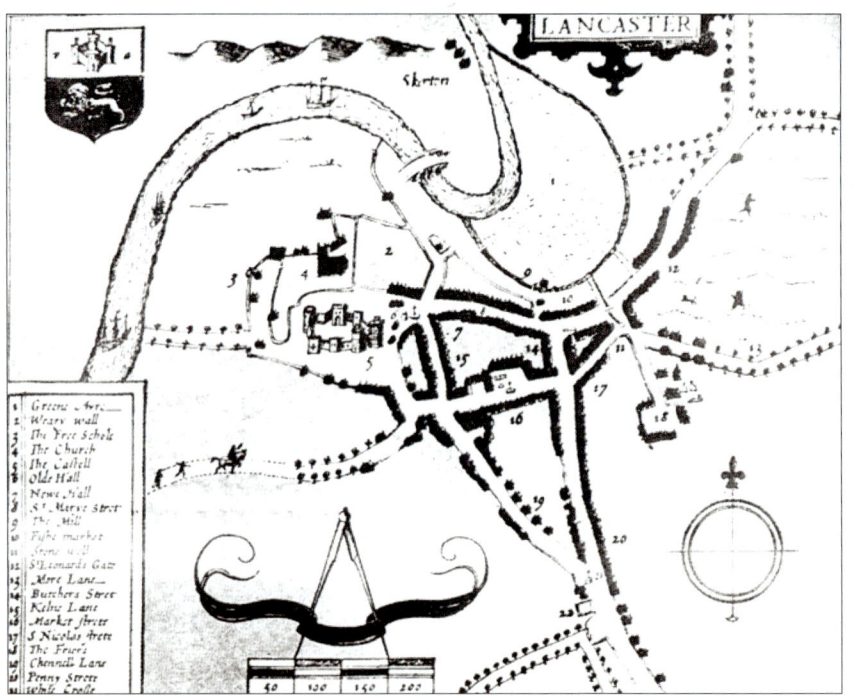

Fig 2: Speed's plan of the city of Lancaster. Lancaster castle is numbered '5', although it is drawn in perspective to emphasise its importance.

Normans in the service of Edward the Confessor during the 1050s: four in Herefordshire and one in Essex. With the Norman Conquest the number of castles increased dramatically and they became a lasting feature of the English landscape.[3] However, the first castle to be built in North West England was not until 1070, when an artificial earthen mound known as a motte, with a wooden tower on the top, was erected at Chester by King William (Fig 1).

Although 21st century North West England encompasses two historic borders (those with north-eastern Wales and south-western Scotland) the 83 castles definitely known within the region account for less than ten percent of the total number of castles recorded in England; a percentage not significantly increased by the identification of a number of undocumented earthwork sites in recent years.[4] This number is based primarily on Cathcart King's index, with amendments where necessary (see Chapter 5). The study of castle sites in the region can, perhaps, be traced to Speed's maps of Cheshire and Lancashire (Fig 2) surveyed in the early-17th century. These included the earliest plans of any of the

The first castle to be built in North West England was not until 1070, when the motte at Chester was erected by King William

> **The earliest Archaeological excavations on a North West castle took place in the 19th century**

castle sites from the region. Antiquarian interest in the 18th century focused upon the dramatic setting of the ruined castles, with the Buck Brothers sketching many of the stone castles of the region in the late-1720s and 1730s (Fig 3). In the late-18th and early-19th centuries castle sites were also the subject of several paintings by landscape artists including John Constable and Joseph Turner as well as local artists such as Moses Griffth.[5]

The earliest archaeological excavations on a North West castle took place in the 19th century with the investigation of the earthworks at Penwortham, near Preston, and Mote Hill to the north of Warrington. Results from these were not very revealing and in some cases have been lost entirely; as with the early investigations at Hornby in the Lune valley.[6]

The 20th century saw an upsurge in interest in the castles of the region with an increasing number of archaeological and historical studies, and a growing list of protected sites (Fig 4). This work included several landscape studies. Cathcart King's monumental survey of the castles of England and Wales, published in 1983,[7] included entries for 78 castles and 86 tower houses in the region with bibliographies for each, although no plans nor elevations were included. As befits their more numerous nature, the castles and tower houses of Cumbria saw three major studies in this century.[8] The less numerous castles of the truncated post-1974 county of Lancashire had three significant studies during this century.[9] The late 20th century metropolitan areas of Liverpool and Manchester have none, and more surprisingly Cheshire also lacks a detailed landscape overview of its castles. Although it has been covered in a gazetteer published in 2001, that work mirrors the studies of Cathcart

Fig 3: Chester Castle and its motte as drawn by Nathaniel and Samuel Buck in 1727.

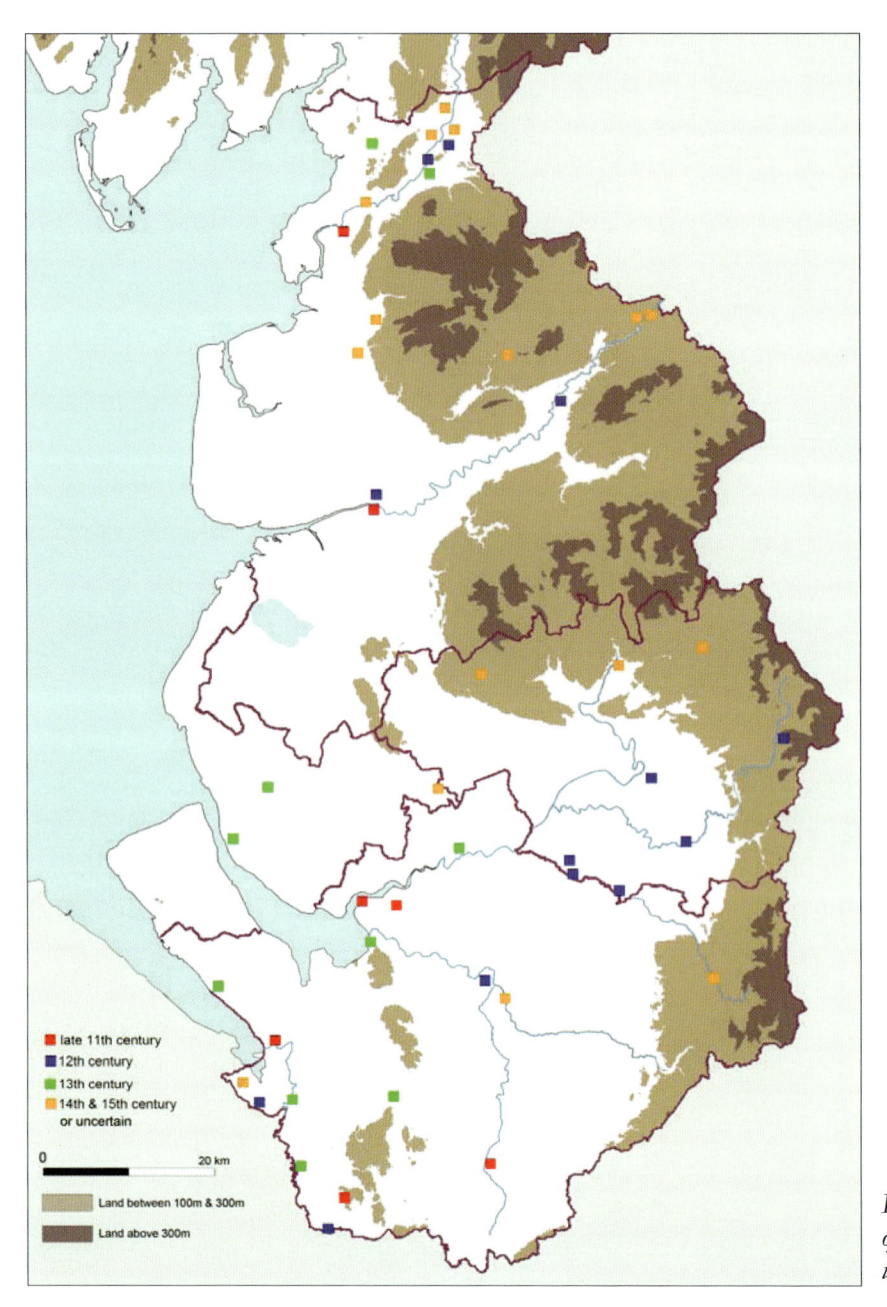

Fig 4: The distribution and date of castles in the southern part of the North West.

King by overlooking Watch Hill near Altrincham and locating Buckton Castle in Lancashire rather than in Cheshire.[10]

Despite the unevenness of the historical studies of North West castles during the 20th century, excavation and survey work during this period encompassed 30 sites. This work ranged from fabric surveys and test pitting to area excavations, with a large bias towards the investigation of stone castles. Archaeological work on earthwork and timber castles often focused on those that developed into important later castles. In Cheshire these were the castles at Aldford and Nantwich. In Greater Manchester small-scale investigations were undertaken on early sites at Watch Hill in 1976, Rochdale in 2001 and at Manchester Castle, in the grounds of Chetham College, in the early 1980s, the latter exposing a possible inner defensive ditch.[11] West Derby[12] was the only earthwork to see significant investigation in the Merseyside area during this period. In Lancashire no mottes were investigated during the 20th century and little archaeological work has been undertaken on Cumbria's northern earth and timber castles. The exception was the major excavations by Davison during the 1960s at Aldingham.[13]

The most extensively investigated stone castle in the region is Beeston in Cheshire (Fig 5). This was the subject of excavations between 1968 and 1985,[14] which showed the outer curtain wall for the early-13th century stone castle was built on the remains of a late-Bronze Age and early-Iron Age hillfort. Elsewhere in the region the stone castles at three of the county towns have been studied. The fabric of Carlisle Castle, and its associated town walls, has been extensively recorded though only parts of the defensive ditch system have been investigated.[15] The stone castles at two other medieval county towns in the region, Chester and Lancaster, have seen only very limited excavation work. Elsewhere in the region the stone castle at Liverpool[16] has seen only small-scale investigation. Halton on the southern side of the Mersey estuary has seen more investigation though this was confined to a series of evaluation trenches.[17] Yet such a limited approach can provide extremely useful results; the location of the late medieval castle at Lathom in southwest Lancashire, which was rebuilt on a palatial scale during the 15th century, has recently been confirmed by just such evaluation work.[18] In Cumbria the stone castles at Brougham, Brough, and Piel[19] have all seen small-scale excavation combined with standing building work. Investigations at the stone castle at Kendal have helped to confirm the

> Archaeological work on earthwork and timber castles often focused on those that developed into important later castles

Fig 5: The outer bailey gateway and curtain wall at Beeston Castle. Beeston was systematically investigated between 1968 and early 1985, and remains the most extensively excavated site in the region.

rather sporadic historical record, although its origins as an earth and timber castle remain uncertain. Other stone castles in Cumbria to receive archaeological attention in the late 20th century include Pendragon, where recording has been undertaken of the upstanding elevations as well as partial clearance of collapsed masonry. Limited recording and excavation work has also taken place at Egremont.[20]

The recent work at Buckton Castle, in Greater Manchester, thus represents the most extensive programme of castle excavation in the

North West, in terms of the percentage of the defences and interior investigated, since the work at Beeston. It also fits into a pattern of research on the stone castles of the region that first began in the 1970s.

The Earliest Castles in North Western England

The first castles in the region were built of earth and timber as motte and bailey types, and have traditionally be assigned to the late-11th and 12th centuries.[21] Many of these early castles acted as both baronial strongholds and estate administrative centres, as well as strategic military installations,[22] although some may have been short-lived.

In Cheshire most of the 13 definite mottes lie in the western third of the county, along the border with Wales, with earth and timber castles known at Aldford, Castleton (Church Shocklach), Chester, Dodleston, Malpas (Fig 6), Pulford and Shotwick. These motte and bailey castles have been considered to belong to the immediate post-Norman Conquest period, though most have not been extensively investigated and where they have, as at Aldford[23] the excavations produced no evidence for occupation before the 13th century. Elsewhere within the county other earthwork castles include Castle Cob, Frodsham, Nantwich, and Northwich which all appear to have been associated with baronial holdings. Chester and Shotwick were both held by the earls of Chester and were rebuilt in stone in the late-12th and 13th centuries.

The Greater Manchester area, which comprises the historic northern fringe of Cheshire and the south-eastern part of ancient Lancashire, has seven earthwork castles, nearly all of which can be associated with baronial holdings. These include the three castles on the northern side of the River Bollin at Dunham, Watch Hill and Ullerwood[24] which were all held by the de Massey family. Despite excavation dating evidence for the motte at Blackrod is lacking. Manchester, first referred to in 1184[25], and Rochdale were the centres of large estates in the 12th century. It is unclear what type of castle was at Stockport when it was mentioned in 1173 but it was probably a motte with a timber tower. Buckton Castle, was not mentioned in the documents until 1360, by which date it was in ruins.[26]

There are two concentrations of earth and timber castles within modern Lancashire. Firstly, there was a scattered line of mottes along the Ribble valley. Secondly, there is a larger group of earthwork and timber

> **Many of these early castles acted as both baronial strongholds and estate administrative centres**

Fig 6: The western edge of the motte at Malpas, looking north-eastwards across the modern town towards Beeston Castle.

castles in the Lune valley.[27] These sites include the well preserved and largely unexplored castles at Halton and Hornby, and the early-12th century castle that preceded the later masonry structure at Lancaster.

Cumbria's mottes are probably later than those further south in the region, since much of this area was not conquered by the Normans until the end of the 11th century, and was in the hands of the Scots during the mid-12th century. It was subject to invasion and raiding throughout the late-12th, 13th and early-14th centuries. The fluctuating border with Scotland during this period probably helped to dictate the distribution of the earth and timber castles in this part of the North

there is a larger group of earthwork and timber castles in the Lune valley

West and in some cases these castles are grouped in pairs in the landscape, either side of the late medieval border, as at Liddel Castle and Liddel Strength.[28] Thus, most of Cumbria's mottes lie close to the Scottish border, though as Newman has pointed out whether they truly represent national defensive lines, or reflect the militaristic and feudal nature and status of the 12th and 13th century landholdings is arguable.[29]

The Stone Castles

> Cumbria's mottes are probably later than those further south in the region

Amongst the 83 castles (Figs 4 & 12) known from the region 44, with the addition of Buckton to Cathcart King's list, were either mottes rebuilt in stone or were stone castles from the very beginning. The lack of extensive excavations on most of these sites means it is difficult to be sure which were the earliest masonry castles, or how many had a timber predecessor. However, documentary material (Fig 7) indicates the 12th and 13th centuries saw extensive rebuilding activity across the region.[30]

The earliest masonry fabric in any North West castle may be the herringbone walling work visible at both Brough and Egremont in Cumbria. The fabric at Brough dates to around 1100, whilst that at Egremont is probably from the 1120s.[31] Elsewhere in Cumbria there are a line of stone castles, including Brougham, Brough, Penrith, and Pen-

Fig 7: The date of the first record of castles in the North West. Three broad phases of activity can be seen; the late-11th to early-12th centuries; the late-12th to late-14th centuries, and the later 15th century. The peak in the 1320s reflects the response to the harrying of northern England by Robert the Bruce of Scotland.

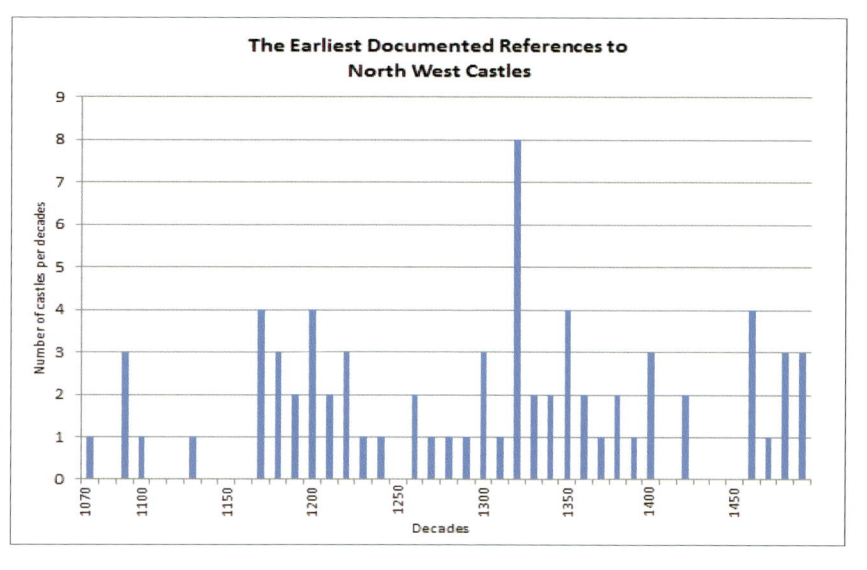

Fig 8: The ruined keep at Brough, which is 12th century, although other parts of the castle may date to c. 1100.

dragon, guarding the upper Eden Valley and the strategic Stainmore pass into north Yorkshire. Norman keeps, probably from the mid- to late-12th century, can be found at Appleby (built around 1130), Brough (Fig 8, Brougham (built around 1200), and Carlisle (Fig 9).[32] The keeps at Appleby, Brough, and Brougham were all raised by a single storey soon after their completion whilst in the 13th century round towers were added to Appleby and Brough.

The two earliest masonry castles in Lancashire are both built on rocky outcrops above river crossings. The first three storeys of the keep at Lancaster are thought to date from *c.* 1130,[33] judging from the survival of round-arched windows with attached shafts and the presence of pilaster buttresses at each corner. Entered from the first floor it had a classic central dividing wall. The upper storey of the keep was added in the 13th century, as at Appleby, Brough, and Brougham. The curtain walls at Lancaster were later and included the surviving Well Tower of *c.* 1265 with its garderobes. The monumental gatehouse with its two octagonal towers was later still, probably being in the early 15th century. Clitheroe Castle (Fig 10) is documented in the first half of the 12th century, but the small stone keep (11m²) is late-12th century in style. Like Lancaster it was entered at first floor level, it also had external

The lack of extensive excavations on most of these sites means it is difficult to be sure which were the earliest masonry castles, or how many had a timber predecessor

> **The two earliest masonry castles in Lancashire are both built on rocky outcrops above river crossings**

chamfering at the base of the corners.[34]

Liverpool Castle, an enclosure castle demolished in 1726, was built in stone around 1235 by William de Ferrers to guard the medieval town. It had a moat and a curtain wall with five D-shaped towers, two of which formed a gatehouse. The main building in the interior was a large stone hall.[35] It has similarities to some of the castles built or rebuilt by Ranulf, sixth earl of Chester, in the earlier 13th century at Beeston (see below), Chester, and Chartley, including the towered gateway and the D-shaped wall towers.

In Cheshire the earliest stone fabric is to be found in the lower two storeys of the Agricola Tower, the original gatehouse to the inner bailey of Chester Castle. This square three-storey tower was begun in the late-12th century by Ranulf, sixth earl of Chester, although the rib-vaulted gateway tunnel was built after a fire in 1302.[36] New inner and outer gateways were added in the early-13th century by Ranulf and each had a pair of D-shaped towers similar to the ones built at Beeston, though the Chester examples were demolished during rebuilding work in the 1800s.[37] Some medieval fabric also survives in the Flag Tower and Half

Fig 9: The keep at Carlisle Castle dates to the 12th century.

Fig 10: The base of the keep at Clitheroe. Note the first floor entrance and the later chamfered corner to the tower base.

Moon Tower, also in the inner bailey.

Elsewhere in the county Halton Castle, possibly established as a motte and bailey in the 1070s by Nigel, the baron of Halton, on the southern bank of the River Mersey, was rebuilt in stone in the 13th century.[38] The inner bailey is formed by the remains of a stone wall, which is thought to be mid-13th century, with a western square tower and a

> **In Cheshire the earliest stone fabric is to be found in the lower two storeys of the Agricola Tower, the original gatehouse to the inner bailey of Chester Castle**

circular tower on the northern side of the bailey. A range of buildings interpreted as a kitchen block are also thought to be 13th century in origin, whilst the outer gateway was rebuilt in the 15th century The inner bailey is often described as a shell keep[39] though the irregular shape of the enclosure does not fit the normal description of such sites.

The best known, certainly the most prominent, of all the castles in Cheshire is Beeston (fig 11). This castle sits atop an outcrop of sandstone dominating the Cheshire plain. It was characterised by an inner and outer bailey with stone defences to the south where the slope did not provide a natural obstacle. Begun in the 1220s by Ranulf, sixth earl of Chester, the design uses its elevated central position to create a dramatically imposing site. The outer and inner gateways each have pairs of D-shaped towers, which are some of the earliest examples in England, and were possibly inspired by Ranulf's knowledge of castles in the eastern Mediterranean from his time on crusade. Seven surviving D-shaped towers line the outer bailey wall. The inner gateway, with its pair of D-shaped banded towers, had a single room above the entrance, a portcullis groove and a pit for a drawbridge. Aside from the gatehouse there are three D-shaped towers distributed between the southern and

Fig 11: The inner bailey at Beeston Castle viewed from the east.

CHAPTER 1 Power, Status and War: The Archaeology of the North West Castle

13

eastern walls of the inner bailey. Discounting what are likely to be temporary structures associated with the building work, no features were discovered within the inner bailey.[40]

There are no above-ground remains for the other stone castles built in Cheshire during the 12th and 13th centuries: Buckton and Shotwick. The form and fabric of Buckton is discussed in detail in Chapter 3. It is uncertain when Shotwick was founded, and although it may have been founded as a motte in the 12th century, by 1240 there was a polygonal stone keep here. It fell into decline in the 14th century when much of the stone fabric appears to have been removed.[41]

Castles in the Landscape: Power & Status

The wider landscape context of the castles of North West England can be seen in several ways. Many sites, especially the earlier mottes, were undoubtedly positioned strategically as part of the initial Norman conquest of the region, and were garrisoned accordingly.[42] The guarding of routeways and river crossings is especially notable in the distribution of mottes in the region. Alford and Pulford lie on the banks of the River Dee, south of Chester, guarding river crossings. Watch Hill in Bowdon guards the Roman river crossing of the Bollin in northern Cheshire, whilst the nearby Ullerwood Castle also guards a crossing of the River Bollin. The motte at Penwortham lies beside a crossing of the Ribble opposite Preston where there was a second motte. Another pair of mottes at Arkholme and Melling (Fig 4) on the river Lune in northern Lancashire guarded a further river crossing, and the motte at Halton further downstream performed a similar function. The motte at Old Tebay, the northern-most of a line of earthworks in the Lune valley, sits by the river and seems to have guarded the routeway up the valley towards the pass at Shap.[43] A line of castles guard the Stainmore pass and the upper Eden Valley (Fig 12) – Appleby, Brough and Brougham. Finally, Liddel Castle sits on the southern bank of the Liddel Water on the late medieval Scottish border. A Scottish castle, Liddel Strength, lay on the opposite bank and both guarded a fording point on the river.

The concentration of castles along the present political frontiers between England and Scotland, and England and Wales in the North West hides a much more complicated political and social position in the Anglo-Norman period. The border of Cheshire and England in the late

The best known, certainly the most prominent, of all the castles in Cheshire is Beeston

Saxon period extended westwards into modern Wales to encompass the coastal territory of Flintshire (Atticross Hundred in the Domesday Book) and the Vale of Clwyd – modern Denbighshire. For much of the two centuries before the final conquest of northern Wales by Edward I in the 1280s, the English-Welsh border lay along the Vale of Clwyd and

Fig 12: The distribution and date of the castles of Cumbria.

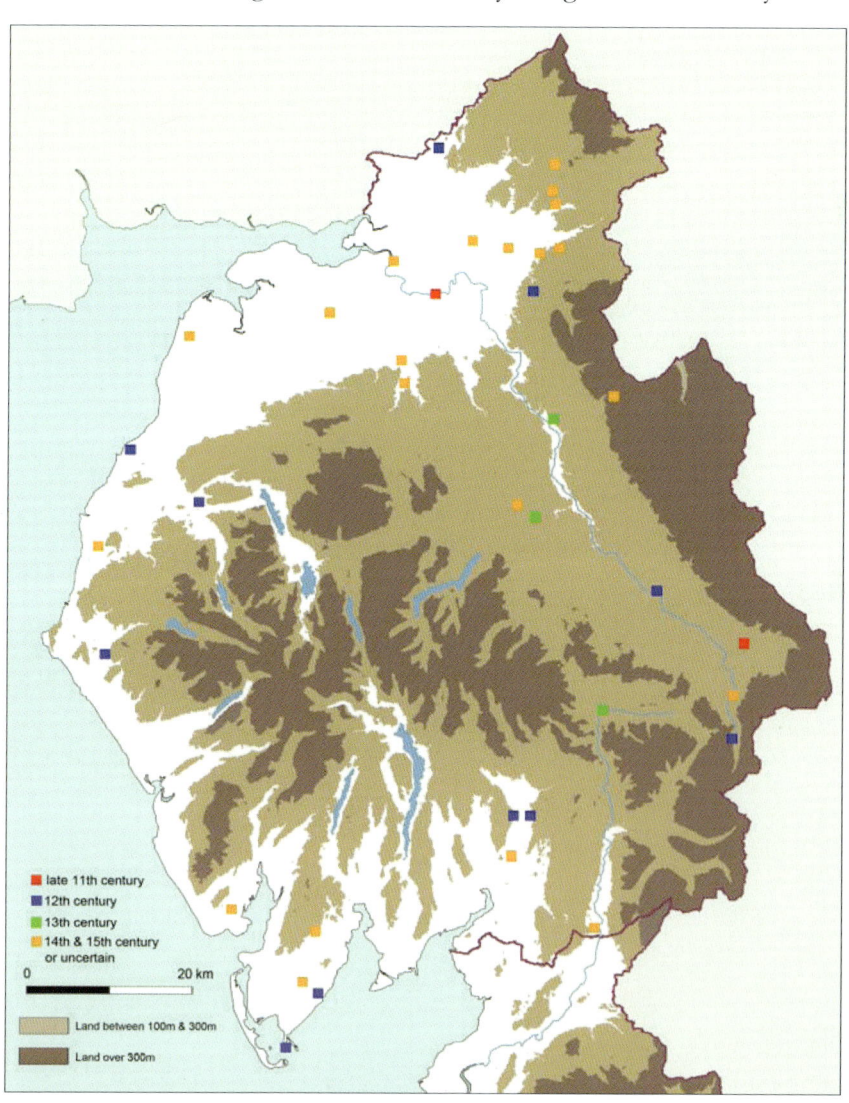

modern north-eastern Wales was part of what might be called Welsh Cheshire. There were exceptions to this Norman dominance. The border was pushed eastwards to the Dee Valley by several Welsh princes; under Owain Gwynedd in the 1140s, by Llewellyn ab Iorwerth in the 1200s, and in the 1260s and 1270s under Llewellyn ap Gruffuth. Richard Newman has suggested the first of these periods of Welsh supremacy might be the context for the building of a series of mottes along the lower Dee valley. Furthermore, he has gone on to suggest this was not a formal frontier but might be interpreted as a series of responses by local Norman lordships to Welsh raids.[44] The sites around Aldford and Pulford appear to be blocking a Welsh raiding route south of the marshes around Saltney for instance, whilst the mottes to the west of Malpas would appear to guard a river crossing of the Dee. None of the mottes along the Dee valley appear to have been rebuilt in stone, probably because the stabilisation of the Welsh frontier by the conquest of Gwynedd at the end of the 13th century removed the strategic need.

The development and defence of the border between England and Scotland was more drawn-out and more complicated than that of the northern Welsh border adjoining Cheshire. Its current position along Liddel Water (Fig 13) was only reached in the 14th century and even then border warfare continued at a low level into the mid-16th century. In the 11th century Cumbria had been part of the British Kingdom of

Fig 13: The motte at Liddel Castle on the Scottish border.

> **Mottes along the Kent and Lune valleys may thus reflect the northern limit of Norman lordship in the late-11th centuries**

Strathclyde; with Carlisle and the Solway plain only falling to William II in 1092. The early mottes along the Kent and Lune valleys may thus reflect the northern limit of Norman lordship in the late-11th centuries. Carlisle Castle was founded around 1092 immediately upon the conquest of the area, whilst the mottes at Kendal (Castle Howe) and at Cockermouth on the western coast date from the early-12th century and perhaps represented the consolidation of landholdings by the Normans.[45] Cumbria remained under Norman control until King Stephen's reign. In 1136 David I invaded northern England in support of his niece Matilda's claim to the English throne, occupying Cumberland, Northumberland, and Westmorland. Scottish possession of the northern counties was confirmed by the Treaty of Durham in 1138 and re-enforced by a second Treaty of Durham in 1139, which saw the lordships of Skipton in north-west Yorkshire and Lancaster pass to Scottish barons.[46] This brought the effective boundary of the Scottish state as far south as the Ribble Valley, where it remained until 1157 when Henry II retook the north through another treaty with the guardians of the new infant Scottish king.[47] It is thus possible that the early mottes of the Ribble Valley (Penwortham, Clitheroe, Ellenthorpe, and Gisburn) might reflect the response of the local Norman lords to the extension of Scottish frontier into northern Lancashire during the period 1136 to 1157.[48]

Yet castles were more than just defensive positions. They acted as baronial and administrative centres, and as social statements of the power and status of their owners. The recognition of their wider role grew with a new wave of studies in the 1990s and 2000s.[49] These studies began to apply landscape and social approaches to castle studies, influenced by archaeological and historical geography methodologies.

The location of early mottes within the ruins of old Roman forts might be indicative of a more symbolic statement of power than just the re-using of an old strategic site with ready building materials to hand; William I's very first castle was built inside the old Roman fort at Pevensey on the Sussex coast.[50] Lancaster Castle, though sited within the defences of the late Roman fortress overlooking the lowest crossing of the river Lune, was also located on a rocky outcrop that dominated the lower part of the valley and the estuary to the west. It was thus a highly visible symbol of late-11th century Norman power in a frontier region. In Cumbria the castles at Appleby, Brough, Brougham (Fig 14),

Power, Status and War: The Archaeology of the North West Castle CHAPTER 1

and Pendragon lie along the strategic routeway into northern Yorkshire from Cumbria through the Stainmore pass, but two of these castles also sit within the earthworks of Roman forts. The motte at Old Tebay sits immediately north of the Roman fort at Low Borrowbridge in the upper Lune Valley. Along the border with Scotland the motte at Beaumont sits on the site of milecastle 70a on Hadrian's Wall, whilst Bewcastle sat within the north-eastern corner of the Roman frontier fort. The building of castles at the old Roman cities of Carlisle and Chester, both of which remained significant urban centres in the 11th century, and both of which lay on river crossings, was probably also a statement of control over the local urban population; a technique frequently used by William I in other English towns (such as Exeter, Lincoln, London, and Norwich) to overawe the Saxon population.[51]

Fig 14 The gateway at Brougham. The castle was built within the earthworks of an old Roman fort.

A further statement of social power was the linking of castles with the church. Carlisle, Chester, and Lancaster each contained private chapels, as did other lesser castles at Appleby, Askham Hall, Bewley, Brougham, Rose Castle in Cumbria, and Dunham in Cheshire. A significant number of castles had churches within the bailey or close by. Chapels within the bailey that later went on to become medieval parish churches can be found at Aldford, Dodleston, and Malpas in Cheshire (Fig 15), at Penwortham in Lancashire, and in Cumbria at Beaumont. Medieval parish churches found immediately outside castles in Cheshire can be seen at Chester, Dodleston, Nantwich, and Stockport. In Lancashire parish churches adjacent to castles included Arkholme, Bury, Lancaster, Manchester, Melling, West Derby, and Whittington. In Cumbria these sites could be found at Bewcastle, Castle Carrock, Irthington, and Kirkoswald, although the fewer examples in this part of region probably represents the lower level of population. Where documentary evidence survives, as at Aldford, Chester, Manchester, and Malpas,[52] it is clear these churches were sponsored by the owners of the castles, an extension of their patronage.

In terms of display and status the building of Beeston Castle in central Cheshire is one of the most imposing examples. Along with Bolingbroke, Allan Brown argues that Beeston is one of the first castles in England to dispense with a central tower, thus beginning a period of scientific fortification. Though principles such as using projecting towers to provide flanking fire had been used at Dover Castle, built by Henry II in the mid-12th century, and Chateau Gaillard, built by Richard I in the latter half of the 12th century (both royal castles and arguably the crowning architectural achievement of their respective kings), it was not until the 13th century that these principles became widespread in England.[53] Beeston Castle was begun by Earl Ranulf III around 1220 using innovative designs which appear to have been inspired by the earl's time of crusade in the 1210s. These features included D-shaped towers for the outer gateway and curtain wall, one of the first instances of this type of design in England, and an elaborated inner gatehouse with two D-shaped tower picked out with coloured horizontal banding reminiscent of the design of the walls of Constantinople.[54] His lands ran from Chester in the west to Lincoln in the east and Leicestershire in the east Midlands. His power base, however, was the earldom of Cheshire and Beeston Castle faced east and south-eastwards overlook-

> **The location of early mottes within the ruins of old Roman forts might be indicative of a more symbolic statement of power than just the re-using of an old strategic site**

ing the main routes from the Midlands. Beeston was a statement of power and status, and perhaps given its design innovations and echo of Constantinople a statement of military ability, reflecting Ranulf's position as the wealthiest landowner in early-13th century England.

Another remarkable statement of power and status can be seen at Lancaster Castle (Fig 16). Its elaborate south-eastern gatehouse was rebuilt after the Scottish raids of 1389. The work was undertaken by Henry, Duke of Lancaster, in the early 15th century but it reflected more than just the need to repair the neglected castle defences. It has two large octagonal towers topped by machicolations and over the gateway itself are two coats of arms flanking a slot for a statue. This appears to have been a visible symbol of Henry's status as earl of Lancaster. He had inherited his estates when his father, John of Gaunt, died in 1399 but these were confiscated by the king upon his death. His son Henry went on to depose Richard and install himself as King Henry IV, thus bringing the earldom of Lancaster into royal hands.[55]

These castles reflected in stone the desire for comfort, wider social interests, and political concerns of two of the biggest landholders of their period. The increasing importance of display and status also

A further statement of social power was the linking of castles with the church

Fig 15: The mediaeval parish church at Malpas lies within the outer bailey of the castle.

Fig 16: The elaborate early 15th century gateway at Lancaster Castle.

marked the beginning of a shift away from the military aspect of castle design, a trend which developed rapidly in the 14th and 15th century.

The Decline of the Castle

The castles built by Edward I in Wales during the late-13th and early-14th century (such as Caernarfon and Beaumaris), are generally held to be the pinnacle of medieval military architecture, and in military terms what follows is an "anti-climax".[56] However, the 14th century saw much castle construction and it was not until the 15th century that construction dramatically dropped off.[57] From the second half of the 14th century, gunloops for the use of gunpowder weapons were incorporated in castle walls, but it wasn't until the development of large, reliable, gunpowder weapons in the 15th century that they became a threat to castle walls.[58] An examination of the licences to crenellate in terms of period in which they were granted offers insights into the changing nature of castle building. The licences were royal grants of permission to build a castle or fortified house and more likely served more as a status symbol – the holder had the right to one of recognised symbols of nobility – rather than planning permission in a modern sense. There were 252 licences were granted between 1300 and 1399, compared to 66 between 1400 and 1499 and 14 between 1500 and 1569.[59] This decline may mark a decrease in the value placed on a licence and the privilege it granted.

The rise of effective gunpowder artillery, controlled by the crown rather than the unruly feudal lords, culminated in the early-16th century with a move towards dedicated forts and fortifications.[60] As the military importance of the castle declined the other functions of these sites, as baronial centres and domestic residences, grew in importance. In the North West this was reflected in the alteration and expansion of domestic ranges, an increase in administrative buildings such as court houses, and the abandonment of some stone castles. These centuries also saw the growth of the fortified manor house.

The rise in importance of the domestic side of castles was foreshadowed by the building of Stokesay Castle (Fig 17) in the 1290s.[61] This had a large four-bay open hall abutting the curtain wall, with a three-storey stone and timber solar wing to the north and a hexagonal four-storey stone tower to the south. The complex was set within a moat but the curtain wall was pierced by windows where the hall range abutted it and the upper floor of the solar range was timber-framed, suggesting the domestic features were of equal importance to the fortified nature of the site.[62]

The improvement of the domestic facilities of stone castles and the rise in importance of display features during the 14th century can be seen at a number of key sites in England. Dunstanburgh Castle (Fig 18), on a headland on the Northumberland coast with its own harbour, is an example of a castle built for both military strength and display. It was built by Earl Thomas of Lancaster between 1313 and *c.* 1322 on the site of a prehistoric fort and had its own harbour to the east and a northern gateway (Lilburn Tower). To the west were built a string of three shallow fresh-water meres. The great gateway to the south had twin three-storey round towers. From the top of these tall turrets projected at

> **The curtain wall was pierced by windows where the hall range abutted it and the upper floor of the solar range was timber-framed**

Fig 17: The building of Stokesay in the 1290s signalled a change in castle design with a move towards more domestic features.

both the southern front and northern rear of the gatehouse. The third floor appears to have contained the main domestic rooms in the castle including a hall and great chamber, which were also accessible from the inner courtyard of the castle.[63] John of Gaunt, fourth son of Edward III, inherited the castle in 1362 and between 1372 and 1383 modernised the structure. He built a curtain wall behind the great gateway to create an inner bailey, added six domestic buildings, including a new bakehouse, and then a new tower and gateway to tightly control access from the outer bailey into the inner bailey. Finally, he built a new gatehouse and barbican *c.* 30m to the west of the original great gateway which was converted into a keep. The castle sat in a wider designed landscape that was used by both Earl Thomas and John of Gaunt. The meres would have given the impression that the castle sat on its own island, with an outer series of defences formed by large earthen banks guiding the visitor across a broad open area to the great gateway with its lofty turrets, reminiscent of Edward I's castles at Caernarfon and Conwy. The castle would thus have dominated the surrounding coast and landscape, acting as a statement of the status and power of its lords.[64]

The primacy of display and comfort over military needs is demonstrated by Bodiam Castle in East Sussex (Fig 19). This was built by Edward Dallyngrigge after 1385 under a licence to crenellate that allowed him to fortify his manor house against French raids. Instead he built a new castle on a new site that was roughly square in plan. The interior was completely occupied by the great hall and its domestic ranges set around the inner walls. These buildings included the lord's hall, a great chamber, chapel, private apartments, kitchen, buttery, pantry, retainer's

Fig 18: The dramatic gateway of Dunstanburgh castle, Northumberland, built between 1313 and 1322 reflects the social pretensions of its builder, Earl Thomas of Lancaster.

hall, and stables. There were three-storey circular towers at each corner of the curtain walls and projecting square central towers in the southern, eastern, and western walls. The main entrance was through the northern gateway that had twin octagonal towers three-storeys high, with gun loopholes, leading to a drawbridge across the moat. Several elements of the castle suggest comfort and display were more important than defence, although its very presence must have acted as a deterrent to the French Channel raiders of this period.[65] Firstly, large windows in the curtain walls provided lighting for these domestic structures. Secondly, the moat was terraced into the hillside on its northern side and damned on its southern side which would have made it very easy to drain in any siege. Thirdly, there were a series of millponds immediately to the south, re-enforcing the impression of the castle sitting on its island within an extensive watery landscape. Finally, the presence of gunloops in the castle may not have been practical, and may have been intended to demonstrate the owner's knowledge of military vocabulary, as it were.[66]

The shift from defence to domestic and display concerns can also be seen at existing castle sites. Warkworth Castle (Fig 20), on the river Aln in Northumberland, was a 12th century motte and bailey with a tower keep, which saw use and development down to the end of the 16th century. It was owned by the Percy family, dukes of Northumberland, the most important noble family in the north, and who were regularly involved in court politics. Here, the keep, sited on the earlier motte, was rebuilt in the late-14th century by Henry Percy, first earl of Northumberland. Its new design illustrates the increasing importance of display and comfort.[67] It was laid out in the form of a Greek cross with four floors. The first storey was used for storage while the second contained the kitchens. The third storey contained the two-storey great hall, a chapel, and a receiving room, with the kitchen range occupying the western side of the floor. The fourth storey housed the bedrooms and withdrawing rooms. Externally, the bailey elevation was dominated by large traceried windows, especially on the third and fourth storeys, and was topped with battlements and beneath these were carvings of angels carrying shields. The north face overlooked the town and was decorated with the Percy lion. A square tower at the northern end of the keep rose two storeys above the main structure, emphasising further the height of the keep by its position on the original motte that stood

Dunstanburgh Castle...is an example of a castle built for both military strength and display

on the edge of the River Aln, which flows in a deep gorge beside this part of the castle. The great hall on the western side of the bailey was rebuilt in the 1480s and the new building included a northern public entrance from the courtyard through the two-storey Lion Tower, with the Percy coat of arms on it.

Amongst the castles of the North West several show signs of conversion to more domestic uses. This usually took the form of the rebuilding and addition of new private apartments and status features such as gateways and battlements, and can be seen at the castles owned by the Clifford family in Yorkshire (Skipton) and Cumbria (Brough and Brougham) during the late medieval period. Brough Castle (Fig 21), in the upper Eden Valley, saw two significant phases of late medieval development. In the 1380s Roger, fifth Lord of Clifford, rebuilt both the southern curtain wall and the two-storey hall range with new large tracery windows in the southern curtain wall. Around 1450 Thomas Clifford built an inner service range on the eastern side of the hall and reinforced the gatehouse with buttresses.[68] Brougham, 18 miles to the north-west, was a 13th century castle that saw a number of late medieval rebuildings and additions. The three-storey gatehouse, with its inner and outer gatehouses and a courtyard in between, was early-14th century. The early 13th century keep was raised by a fourth storey at the same time. The great hall south-east of the keep was rebuilt in the late-14th century with large traceried windows. At Cockermouth on the Cumbria coast Thomas de Lucy built a new hall range with solar and kitchen on the north-western side of the inner bailey around 1360. This too involved punching large window openings into the earlier curtain wall.[69]

Piel Castle, on an island off the southern coast of the Furness peninsula, was built in the late medieval period and incorporates the domestic and display features seen elsewhere in the north. A licence to crenellate the site was granted in 1327 to John Cockerham, abbot of Furness. The castle was probably used to protect the abbey from sea-borne raids into Barrow harbour[70] and much of the fabric is thought to date from the 14th and 15th centuries. The site is dominated by a keep on a cliff edge, which is enclosed to the south and east by an inner and outer bailey, each with their own ditch. The massive three-storey keep has angled corner buttresses and, unusually, two spine walls instead of one, dividing it into three parallel sections. Private apartments occupied the

The primacy of display and comfort over military needs is demonstrated by Bodiam Castle in East Sussex

Fig 19: Bodiam Castle, built in the 1380s, looks impregnable but the moat was terraced into the hillside and the castle overlooked by neighbouring hills. It was more for show than defence.

upper two floors; these were lit by large windows that give the keep a domestic appearance.

The last purpose-built castle in the region shows both these castle design developments (more prominent domestic buildings and display elements). Penrith Castle was built by Ralph Neville on a hill overlooking the town, after he had been granted the manor of Penrith in 1396. He appears to have built the moat and drawbridge, crenellated curtain wall, two-storey gatehouse, and a range of apartments, including a great hall, along the north-eastern and south-eastern sides of the enclosure. His son Richard Neville built the three-storey red tower in the north-western corner of the compound around 1430. The castle was granted to Richard, duke of Gloucester, later King Richard III (1483-85), in

Fig 20: Warkworth in Northumberland had a keep that was a late medieval great house.

1470. He undertook significant alterations to the castle, which were focussed upon domestic accommodation and display. New heated domestic buildings were constructed along the north-western and south-western sides of the courtyard. To light the new private apartments large windows were inserted in the curtain wall. Finally, a new outer gatehouse to enhance the north-western approach to the site, was built over the moat.[71]

The trend towards display and status can also be seen in the fortified manor houses of the region, which began to emerge during the 14th century. Their construction reflected not only the continued insecurity of the northern frontier with Scotland but also the wealth and competition within and between the late medieval landed elite. These fortified manor houses were characterised by a three- or four-storey square-plan stone tower at one end of an open medieval hall. Many of these late medieval sites had licences to crenellate from the king. In Cheshire two licences were given in the 14th century, for Doddington Hall in 1364 and Macclesfield Castle in 1398. Within historic Lancashire five licences are known, all from the 15th century; Thurland Castle in 1402, Radcliffe Tower in 1403, Stanley Tower in 1406, Bury Castle in 1469, and Greenhalgh Castle in 1490.[72] Cumbria had 18 sites with licences to crenellate, which is than double the number to be found in Cheshire and Lancashire combined[73] emphasising its closer position to the unstable Scottish border. Of these licences 13 dated to the period 1307-36, a period of intense warfare between England and Scotland. During the reign of Robert the Bruce between 1306 and 1329 the Scots raided deep into northern England, burning manors and villages as far south as northern Yorkshire and central Lancashire.[74] The remaining five Cumbrian licences to crenellate came from later in the 14th century.

The trend towards display and status can also be seen in the fortified manor houses of the region

Bury Castle, with a licence to crenellate in 1469, was another 15th century site with a large central tower on a substantial rectangular, buttressed platform surrounded by a moat. However, many other defended sites did not have a licence. Along the Lune Valley to the northeast of Lancaster the line of early motte and bailey castles were replaced in the 14th and 15th centuries by a series of fortified manor houses with stone towers, at Ashton, Borwick, Hornby, and Thurland.[75] Whilst further north dozens of pele towers, defended stone refuges for farming families, were built in the 15th and 16th centuries in response to the activities of the border reevers – livestock raiders. The largest and most elaborate of the late medieval fortified manors of the region was Lathom House in western Lancashire. This was built by Thomas Lord Stanley in the period 1459-1504. It had a central keep, two courts, eleven towers, and a double moat,[76] but was demolished after the First Civil War in 1646, so its grandeur can only be recovered by archaeological work. The scale of the central keep may have been influenced by the design of Penrith Castle.[77]

Several other trends in the development of the stone castles of the region can also be seen. Some fell into decline and ruin. In Cheshire Buckton Castle was a ruin by 1360 and Shotwick fell into decline at the end of the 14th century. Stockport Castle had been partly built over by the expanding market town by the 16th century.[78] Beeston Castle, however, appears to have been maintained by the Crown.[79]

Yet the defences of a number of northern castles were improved in the 14th century. At Clitheroe a new outer bailey gateway was built in 1324; at Brougham the curtain wall was repaired and a round tower added in 1319; and the outer gatehouse at Carlisle was rebuilt in 1378. This rebuilding work probably reflected the continuing threat of war and the chronic instability of the border with Scotland.

A shift towards administrative functions can be seen at other castle sites. Halton was used as a courthouse and prison from 1423 onwards and a new outer gatehouse with polygonal towers, like those at Lancaster, was built in the 1450s, the present courthouse was built in 1723. The courthouse at Clitheroe Castle was added even later, being erected in the early 19th century. Two other castles in the region retained an administrative function into the post-medieval period; Chester and Lancaster. Chester Castle had a major administrative and symbolic function from its initial construction in 1070-1. Improvements under the Crown during the later 13th and 14th centuries included the building of substantial accommodation for both the constables and the Royal family and a new court house.[80] Lancaster Castle developed a role as a prison and court from the early-19th century. Like Chester, this led to the demolition and rebuilding of a significant part of the castle and has hampered the later archaeological study of the complex. Nevertheless, there is extensive evidence for the castle's refurbishment during the late-14th and early-15th century which included the rebuilding of the elaborate outer bailey gateway.[81]

Henry VIII's coastal fortifications of the 1530s and 1540s marked the end of traditional castle building in Britain and the emergence of forts.[82] Sites such as Camber Castle in East Sussex and Deal Castle in Kent were gun-emplacements with an interleaving circular-tower plan and moats with raked sides designed to absorb cannon fire. These forts, with their squat towers, were visually quite different from the classic medieval castle. Even though they contained accommodation blocks in the central tower[83] they were quite clearly different to the medieval castle in their function and design.[84] They were no longer defended residences but fortifications under royal control. In North West England this transition from castle to fort can be seen at Carlisle (Fig 22) where

The largest and most elaborate of the late medieval fortified manors of the region was Lathom House in western Lancashire

Fig 21: The 14th century round Clifford tower and great hall at Brough, Cumbria.

the defences were refurbished during the 1540s. At the castle a half-moon battery was built in front of the inner gatehouse, the Captains' Tower, whilst the southern gateway into the walled city was rebuilt as a triangular gun redoubt formed by three towers linked by short curtain walls, later known as The Citadel.[85]

Beyond the Castle Gate

Although medieval castle sites in the region are not numerous, the North West offers a unique opportunity to examine such sites in two border areas. Two recently suggested lines of research both relate to this topographical position; firstly, how do the castles in these border areas compare with each other and if they differ why do they? Secondly, how much of a response to a frontier location were these castles, or were they simply a product of the local feudal hierarchy and its requirements?[86]

Fig 22: The half moon gun battery built at Carlisle Castle in the 1540s in front of the inner gateway marked the end of classic forms of medieval castle design in the North West.

A third line of enquiry might be how far the chronological spread of castle building and refortification in the North West was influenced by the bouts of civil war within the ruling nobility during the Medieval period. The three main eras of instability most relevant to the region are the 'Anarchy' of King Stephen's reign (1136-54), the barons' revolt of 1173, and the Wars of the Roses during the mid-15th century.

Other more specific archaeological research issues await investigation. For instance are the mottes in the southern part of the region generally earlier than those in the north? How many castles now classified as earthworks were actually stone built from their foundation? How many of the stone castles overlie primary earth and timber fortifications? When was the transition from earth and timber to stone at these sites and how many of the 16th and 17th century great houses of the North West developed from earlier castle sites?[87] For a monument type that remains a prominent feature in the North West landscape, and on which a great deal of research has already been undertaken over the last two centuries, there remains much still to understand and record. The recent work at Buckton Castle is a small contribution towards this understanding.

The North West offers a unique opportunity to examine such sites in two border areas

Fig 23: Peveril Castle, northern Derbyshire, was built by one of the rivals to the earls of Chester in the 12th century.

Chapter 2

The Political and Social Context of Buckton

Introduction

The remains excavated at Buckton Castle appear to belong to the 12th or 13th centuries (see below Chapter 3). Since there were no other powerful lords in eastern Cheshire during this period it is therefore highly likely that the castle was built by one of the earls. Therefore in order to understand the medieval context of Buckton it is necessary to look at the role of the earls of Chester in the region (Fig 23).

The Earls of Chester

The earls were amongst the most important castle builders in North West England. The earldom itself was established by William the Conqueror, founder of Chester Castle in 1070, when he made his nephew Hugh (I) d'Avranches earl of Chester shortly afterwards.[1] The title and associated holdings descended through Hugh's heirs until 1237 when the earldom was taken over by the Crown.[2] However, the power of the earls of Chester extended beyond the borders of the county: "the strength and importance of the great independent earls of Chester between 1071 and 1237 did not rest upon palatine rights or special status, but upon the very extensive lands of the honour of Chester, spreading into numerous counties, and the vast influence and wealth that these gave to them".[3] According to the Domesday Survey of 1086, the value of the earl's holdings in Cheshire amounted to 25.7 per cent of the total of his holdings across England. While he held land in 21 counties only two amounted for more than 8.0 per cent of the total value: Lincolnshire (20.0 per cent) and Suffolk (11.9 per cent).[4]

Cheshire was not a wealthy county and based upon the evidence from the Domesday Survey it was clearly "one of the least developed parts of the Norman realm". The value of the Domesday manors of the county

> **The earls were amongst the most important castle builders in North West England**

decrease across Cheshire the further east they are; only twelve were assessed at £3 or over, and five of these were located in the Dee Valley.[5] Much of the first earl's power came from consistently supporting the king. Though Cheshire was along the Anglo-Welsh border (and was the base for expeditions into north Wales) it was here that Hugh d'Avranches halted the advance of King Malcolm II of Scotland in 1091.[6] When Hugh died in 1101 his heir, Richard, was seven-years-old so Henry I became the boy's guardian. He exercised direct control over the earl's property even after Richard came of age. Richard died in 1120 and was succeeded to the earldom by his cousin, Ranulf (I) de Maschines. Like his predecessors, the new earl was loyal to the king. He was earl of Carlisle through his wife and had extensive holdings in northern England, but was forced to relinquish the earldom of Carlisle when he assumed that of Chester. When he died in 1129 his son, Ranulf (II) de Gernon, became earl.[7] Before 1129 little documentation survives relating to the earl's activities and so identifying which castles belonged to the earls is problematic. The issue is exemplified by the distribution of the earls' charters compiled by Barraclough: of the 437 charters identified, only 15 were issued between 1070 and 1129.[8]

Ranulf de Gernon was politically active and during the civil wars of King Stephen's reign changed allegiances several times. In 1140 he captured Lincoln Castle from Stephen[9] and at the time of his death in 1153 had seized several castles in support of Henry Plantagenet, later Henry II.[10] Though the earl held several castles in this period it was on a temporary basis and Henry took control of them after Ranulf de Gernon died (fig 24).

Hugh (II) de Kevelioc succeeded his father, but in 1153 was still a child.[11] As a consequence, King Henry II took control of the earldom until 1162.[12] The *Cartae Baronum* indicates that in 1166 Hugh de Kevelioc was amongst the four richest earls in England,[13] and as such when Henry II's sons rebelled in 1173 the earl of Chester's decision to support them was important. The earl was captured in Normandy and Chester Castle confiscated, though it was later returned to him when the two reconciled.[14] This contrasts with the fortunes of Robert Blanchemains, earl of Leicester, who was also captured by Henry II and had at least four of his castles slighted. The proximity of Chester to the Anglo-Welsh border and Hugh's contrition probably contributed towards his lenient treatment.[15] The earl died in 1181 and his son Ranulf

Ranulf de Gernon was politically active and during the civil wars of King Stephen's reign changed allegiances several times

(III) de Blundeville inherited. He took up arms against Prince John in 1194 during Richard I's absence, and when the king returned to England he joined other magnates in subduing John.[16] In 1198 he inherited the honour of Bolingbroke, complete with its castle, from William de Roumare.[17] Though the two had previously been at odds, when John became king in 1199 the earl of Chester gave him his support, and during the crisis of John's reign which led to Magna Carta Ranulf de Blundeville stayed loyal to the Crown. He acquired the honours of Leicester and Lancaster in 1215 and 1216 respectively, and in 1217 became earl of Lincoln.[18] In 1218 he embarked on a pilgrimage which eventually

Fig 24: Lands held or claimed by the earls of Chester in north-east Wales and North West England during the 12th century. The location of castles built by the earls in the 12th and early-13th centuries is also shown.

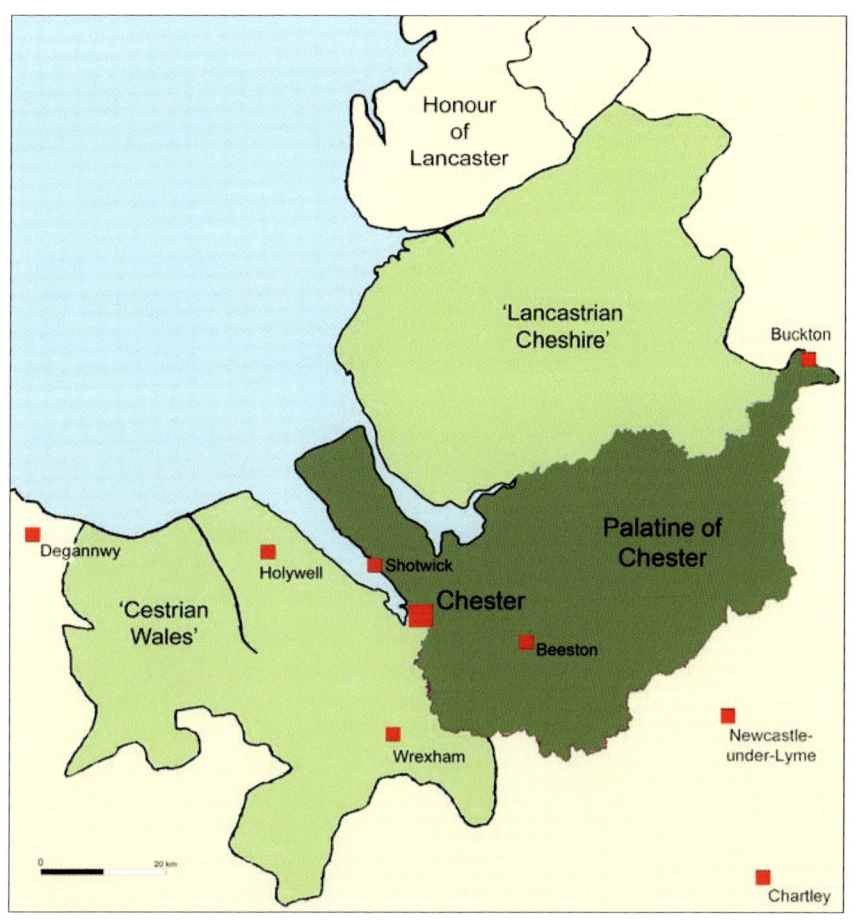

became a crusade. On his return to England in 1220 the previously influential earl rebelled against Hubert de Burgh who ruled on behalf of Henry III while the latter was a minor. Threatened with excommunication, Ranulf abandoned plans to overthrow Hubert[19] and chancery rolls show he surrendered three royal castles he held on behalf of the king and their associated sheriffdoms: Bridgnorth and Shrewsbury in Shropshire, and Lancaster in Lancashire.[20] The earl died in 1232 without children so his nephew, John the Scot, assumed the title. When John died in 1237 Henry III permanently took the earldom under royal control.[21]

The Earls' Castles

In his survey of documentary evidence relating to the castles of England and Wales during the Angevin period (1154–1216), R. Allen Brown asserted that Bolingbroke (Lincolnshire) from 1198[22] and Chester (Cheshire) were the only two castles in England under the direct control of the earls of Chester. However, this survey also showed that further castles in Wales were under the control of the earls (Fig 24). In the 1160s they held Hosely in Flintshire and Wrexham in Denbighshire.[23] Earl Ranulf de Blundeville built Holywell in Flintshire in 1210 and rebuilt Degannwy Castle in Caernarfonshire. According to local tradition Shotwick was built by Hugh (I) d'Avranches in the 11th century, though this is speculative. The stone castle is first documented in 1240 but may predate this and perhaps replaced an earthwork castle. The lack of information about the castle under the earls of Chester means it cannot be satisfactorily included here.[24]

In the Angevin period, Bolingbroke in Lincolnshire was the earl's only major castle outside Cheshire. Tradition has it there was a castle on the site (about 30m above sea level) in the mid-12th century. The stone castle, of which the ruins are today visible, has been dated to the 1220s. At this time Ranulf de Blundeville had returned from the crusades and was building castles at Beeston (Fig 26) and Chartley.[25] Further castles were held by people under the authority of the earls of Chester (Fig 25: Chartley, Staffordshire was held by Ferrers, the Earl of Derby, during 1154-1170 and then Beachamp of Lammarsh from 1170; Dunham Massey, Cheshire by de Mascis; Hawarden, Flint by Montalt; Mold in Flint by Montalt during 1154-99; Prestatyn in Flint by Banastre during 1154-67; Pulford Cheshire by the barons of Pulford; and Uller-

In the Angevin period, Bolingbroke in Lincolnshire was the earl's only major castle outside Cheshire

Fig 25: Castles in the lands held by the earls of Chester, 1070-1237.
Key: 1 - Buckton
2 - Dunham
3 - Hawarden
4 - Mold
5 - Pulford
6 - Ullerwood

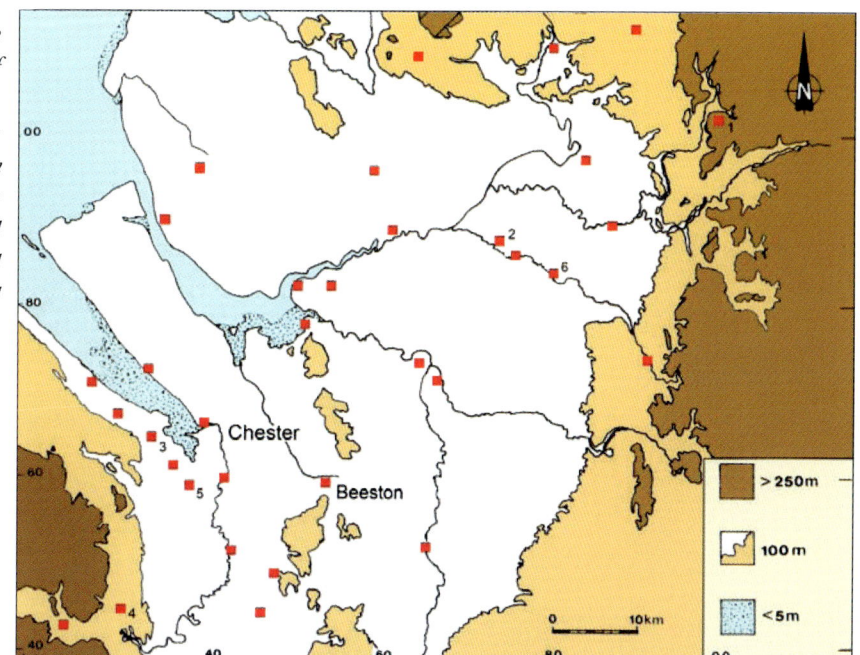

wood in Cheshire in 1173 by de Masci (Fig 25).

Appleby Castle in Westmorland was founded between 1100 and 1120 by Ranulf (I) de Maschines and was taken into royal control in 1120-21. The earls of Chester also held Newcastle-under-Lyme Castle at various times. Located on the Cheshire-Staffordshire border it was originally a royal castle that was granted to the earl of Chester in 1149, but reverted to the Crown four years later when the earl died. In 1215 it was granted to the earl until he died in 1232 when it was given to Gilbert de Segrave.[26] Neither of these castles was held by the earls for an extended period.

Though he was one of the most powerful magnates in England, the Domesday Survey shows that towards the end of the 11th century the earl's urban properties were focused mainly in Chester, with a few in other towns.[27] Of the 36 castles known to have been founded by William the Conqueror, exactly two thirds were in or nearby existing towns.[28] This emphasises the importance of controlling centres of population after the initial Norman Conquest. With relatively few urban centres under the earl's control, it can be expected that a correspond-

Fig 26: The inner ditch at Beeston Castle. The inner bailey wall can be seen on top of the cliff to the left. Much of the stonework used to build the castle, which dominates the skyline of central and southern Cheshire, came from this ditch area.

ingly small number of castles would be under the earl's control, at least soon after the Norman Conquest.

The Castles of Cheshire

Of the 23 castles in Cheshire (Fig 25) as identified by Cathcart King's *Castellarium Anglicanum*, Doddington and Macclesfield were built after 1270, thus falling outside the remit of this chapter. Others may too, but the documentation is unclear, for instance the construction date of the stone castle at Frodsham is uncertain. For many other sites the dates of foundation and use are a matter of speculation. As a result, it is an informed guess that the motte and bailey castles close to the Welsh border date from the 11th or 12th centuries (see above Chapter 1). The problem regarding documentation is illustrated by the case of Frodsham Castle, for which no sources documenting building work survive from before the 15th century.[29]

Some amendments could be made to King's list. Buckton is erroneously given as being part of Lancashire, and Watch Hill is omitted, possibly due to confusion with nearby Ullerwood. Though the figures could be tweaked, the density is one castle to every 40.6 square miles.[30] Excluding towers and artillery forts from the statistics, which do not occur in Cheshire,[31] the density of Westmorland and Cumberland is 56.3 and 71.7 square miles per castle respectively.[32] With the same conditions, the figures for Durham and Northumberland are 56.4 and 35.1 square miles per castle.[33] While Cheshire does not seem exceptional when compared to England's northern border counties, it stands out in comparison to those along the Anglo-Welsh border. In Herefordshire and Shropshire there is on average one castle for every 9.1 and 12.0 square miles respectively.[34]

King proposed two reasons for Cheshire standing out compared to Shropshire and Herefordshire: firstly the disputed border area lay further west than the present border between England and Wales, in the county of Flint, and secondly "the policy of the Palatine Earls".[35] Licences to crenellate gave lords permission to build castles, although the disparity between the number of castles in England and the number of known licences suggests permission was not compulsory.[36] This may be due to the earl's authority and the status of Cheshire as a palatine county. The king usually issued licences to crenellate, but in palatine counties the ruler had this authority. Only five such licences were granted in Cheshire, and eight in Durham (another palatine county). This contrasts with 433 issues by the Crown between 1199 and 1567.[37] Applicants were rarely refused by the king,[38] and the earls of Cheshire may have exercised stricter control over who built castles. The five licences issued to properties in Cheshire cover the period 1364 to 1487,[39] after Wales became part of England and when the county was held by the Crown.

Another consideration which may explain the low number of castles in Cheshire may be that the area was economically under-developed.

> **For many [castles] the dates of foundation and use are a matter of speculation**

With fewer centres of commerce, population, and production there may have been less need for lords to impose their authority. The border counties of Cumberland and Westmorland were equally underdeveloped and have a comparable density of castles.

Aside from those owned by the earl and those under him, two further castles, Halton and Stockport, are documented in Cheshire in 1154–1216.[40] It is assumed that Halton Castle was founded in about 1071 by Nigel, the first baron of Halton.[41] The only medieval reference to Stockport comes from 1173 when Geoffrey de Constentin held it against Henry II.[42] While Stockport appears to have been unimportant, Halton Castle was rebuilt in stone perhaps from the 12th century onwards.[43]

The Location of Buckton

Castles show great variety in their design of castles and in their locations. This was partly because they filled a range of roles. There was no ideal situation for a castle, and a variety of factors would have been considered when choosing where to build. Buckton Castle (Fig 25) occupies a site some 335m above sea level (AOD),[44] and has commanding views to the west and north. On a clear day it is possible to see Beeston Castle from Buckton. The Pennine moorlands rise to the north, east and south-east of Buckton with heather moorland and blanket peat surrounding the site.[45] Of the other castles owned by the Earls of Chester, only Beeston on a sandstone crop 150m AOD, some 110m above the Cheshire Plain, is in a comparably elevated position. Most of the castles in Cheshire are concentrated near the Anglo-Welsh border and Buckton's siting is unusual. It lies in an area that was poor relative to the rest of the county.[46]

Castles on rocky peaks such as Beeston and Buckton, and Peveril in Derbyshire, are a minority of sites.[47] Liddiard points out that such sites have influenced the popular images of castles, and "Dramatically sited above the Cheshire plain, Beeston meets all our preconceptions of what a real castle should look like".[48]

Creighton notes "Although in terms of immediate setting, a castle may appear located relative to particular geographical features, such as a river crossing, fording-place or crossroads of communication routes, in a wider sense, the building of a castle was related, first and foremost, to

Castles on rocky peaks such as Beeston and Buckton, and Peveril in Derbyshire, are a minority of sites

the ownership and control of territory".[49] As highland sites of this sort were uncommon in England it may be fruitful to compare it to a similar case nearby. The 11th century Peveril Castle is located on a limestone ridge at the western end of the Hope Valley (a major line of communication) and it has been suggested that the control of resources, specifically mining, and the manor of Hope were key factors in deciding to build the castle. The symbolism of such a prominent position should also be considered as any building on this site would have been highly visible.[50]

The Domesday Survey shows that in 1086 Hugh d'Avranches held eight manors in and around the Longdendale valley, including those of Tintwistle, Mottram, and Hollingworth.[51] In the medieval period settlement in what would later constitute Tameside was sparse, with fewer than 40 such sites recorded.[52] That being the case, it seems unlikely the location of Buckton Castle was chosen to control the local population or an important economic centre. While Cheshire was under-developed economically, within the county Tameside was one of the poorest areas. This would have been exacerbated in the eastern part where moorland begins.[53]

The Cost and Building Materials of Buckton

Buckton Castle is a stone castle but, as a general rule, the first castles in England were of earth and timber construction. There are only a few examples of castles with 11th-century masonry. This was because a timber structure was quick to erect, and there was plenty of Saxon labour on hand to dig the ditch and pile up the earth for the motte. However, such earth and timber castles could not withstand a prolonged or concerted siege. Of the earliest known castles using stone in England, many were on rocky sites, and building material would have been close at hand, particularly Corfe in Dorset, Peveril in Derbyshire, Ludlow in Shropshire, and Chepstow in Monmouthshire. In the 12th century stone became more common as a building material and many timber castles had their defences rebuilt.[54] Buckton is a high, rocky site, and most of the vegetation in the immediate area is heather, so the availability of timber for construction might have been a factor in why Buckton Castle was built from stone.

Peat samples from Featherbed Moss, 10km to the south-east of

On a clear day it is possible to see Beeston Castle from Buckton

Buckton, provide the best palaeo-environmental data for the Tameside area after the Roman period. In the period between *c.* 740 and 850 AD, tree pollen made up 52 per cent of the pollen recovered; between *c.* 850 to 1459 AD this proportion of tree pollen dropped to 18 per cent with the 9th and 11th centuries recording extensive woodland clearance.[55] It seems possible that a paucity of timber in the area was a factor in Buckton Castle's construction; however, building in stone was more expensive than timber and took a lot longer.

The cost of building castles in the Middle Ages is a tricky subject.[56] A multitude of factors dictated cost, but the most important was the building material and in broad terms building a stone castle was far more costly than building an earth and timber castle. Few records survive relating to the cost of the latter type. Since the work of digging and creating earthworks could be done by any able-bodied person, the skill lay in directing, labour costs would be much less than when masons were required. Workers could notionally have been forced to work for free. Tom McNeill notes that Clones Castle in Ireland cost £20 to build in 1211, of which half was spent on diggers and a quarter on carpenters. He seems to believe this represents the upper cost of a timber and earthwork castle because it is unlikely the local peasantry were forced to do the work so labour had to be imported.[57]

In contrast, R. Allen Brown estimated that during King John's reign a first rate castle might cost more than £7,000, while a "medium castle of reasonable strength might be built for less than £2,000". McNeill broadly agrees with these figures, though casts the net a bit wider, giving £1,000 as a minimum, while estimating that a state-of-the-art castle in around 1200 would cost in the region of £10,000.[58] Even the smallest stone structure was far more costly than building an earth and timber castle. The small keep of Peveril Castle (Figs 23 & 28), 12m square and 16m high,[59] cost £184 in 1175–1177.[60] To put this into context, Sidney Painter estimated the income of Roger de Lacy, the constable of Chester and one of the richest men in England during King John's reign, was about £800 per year. Including Roger de Lacy, only seven barons around 1200 had an income which regularly exceeded £400 per year; of the 54 barons he looked at the median income was £115, while the mean was £202.[61]

So what does the use of stone at Buckton mean? As the earliest surviving reference to Buckton Castle comes from the survey of Longden-

It seems possible that a paucity of timber in the area may have been a factor in Buckton Castle's construction

dale in 1360, we have no direct evidence for how much construction cost. Immediately east of the castle is a modern sandstone quarry, the produce of which has been used in buildings of nearby villages, and it is likely the medieval builders may have used the grey gritstone hacked from the ditch to erect the castle's walls.[62] At Beeston the sandstone cut from the ditch surrounding the inner ward was used in this manner to build the castle,[63] and having a readily available building material would have reduced transport costs (Fig 27).

Although there are no records to show how much it cost to build Buckton, the documented cost for the construction of Peveril Castle, built in 1175-1177 in neighbouring Glossopdale provides a useful parallel. Modelling the keep of Peveril Castle as a regular shape allows an

Fig 27: The c. 2.8m wide curtain wall to the north-east of the gatehouse at Buckton, excavated in 2008. This was a wider structure than the curtain wall at the contemporary Peveril Castle.

estimate of how much stone was used in construction. A solid with a base 12m² and 16m high has a volume of 2,304m³. The cavity inside measures approximately 6.5m by 5.8m by 13.1m, so the rough volume of the keep is 1,810m³. For ease of calculation windows have been ignored.

Buckton Castle is an irregular ellipse (Fig 30), but if we take a regular oval as a model we can begin to work out how much stone was used in the curtain walls. The major axis measured from the external face of the curtain walls is 35.6m, while the minor axis is 26.2m and the walls are 2.8m thick.[64] The walls therefore occupy an area of roughly 247m². For simplicity this estimate does not include the gatehouse, which marked the entrance of the castle. The profile of trench 3 from the 2007 excavations shows the walls extend to a depth of 1.7m below ground level in that spot.[65]

The other variable is the height of the curtain wall. The inner enclosure of Clitheroe Castle (Fig 30) may provide a useful analogy: elliptical in shape, the major axis is aligned east to west and measures 31.8m

Fig 28: Peveril Castle, in northern Derbyshire, was built around the same time as Buckton Castle, but architectural features such as this round Norman arch have not been found at Buckton.

> **Buckton Castle's curtain wall may have needed roughly 1,037m³ of stone**

from the outer face of the curtain walls. The 2.4m thick curtain wall does not entirely encircle the ward and there is a gap in the south, just east of the keep, but measuring the minor axis from the outer face of the north curtain wall to the south corner of the keep gives a figure of 26m. From ground level inside the enclosure to the wall walk on top of the curtain wall is 2.5m.

Excluding the gatehouse, the above suggests Buckton Castle's curtain wall may have needed roughly 1,037m³ of stone. The pipe rolls show £184 was spent at Peveril across 1175–1176 and 1176–1177 on building the keep. With Buckton's curtain walls requiring about 57 per cent of the stone needed for Peveril's keep, we can expect costs to have decreased by a similar proportion. If the median income of barons in 1200 was £115, the theoretical £105 spent at Buckton would have represented a significant investment but would have been within the means of most barons. Someone of the wealth of the earl of Chester would easily have been able to fund the work.

As the expenditure at Peveril lasted two years, it may be inferred that so did the majority of the building work. However, the spending was not evenly split between the two years, £135 in the first year and £49 in the second. Thus, in theory the curtain walls at Buckton Castle could have been built within a single building season.[66]

The Plan-Form of Buckton

Buckton Castle is a single, roughly elliptical enclosure. Before the 21st century excavations, the earthworks were measured at 45m by 35m. This can now be revised. The major axis is aligned north-west to south-east, while the minor axis is oriented south-west to north-east, measuring 35.6m and 26.2m respectively taking the outer face of the curtain walls as start and end points. This means Buckton Castle covers an area of about 730m².[67] A ditch about 10m wide and cut into the bedrock surrounds the castle on all sides apart from the south-west, where the natural slope of the hill renders it unnecessary. At least some of the material from the ditch was deposited within the castle, raising the ground level by 1.5m.[68] Excavations have revealed the castle was enclosed by a sandstone wall 2.8m thick.[69] It is interesting to note the White Tower of the Tower of London, the second largest keep in England, measures 35m by 29m at its base excluding the projections of the apse and corner towers, meaning Buckton would almost have fitted inside its footprint.[70]

The site was accessed through a gatehouse in the north-west corner; the gatehouse, gate-passage, and causeway across the ditch were excavated in 2008 and 2010. The gatehouse measured 7.5m north-west to south-east; the front was level with the outer edge of the curtain wall and measured 9.3m. The south-west end of the gatehouse was occupied by a single room at ground floor level, possibly a guardroom, measuring 3.3m by 6.3m internally, with the shorter axis aligned south-west to north-east; the walls were not uniformly thick, varying from 0.5m to 0.9m. The thicker walls formed part of the gate-passage and the castle's outer walls, while the thinner walls faced the interior of the castle. Immediately north-east of the guardroom was a gate-passage 3.3m wide. It is thought that on the north-east side of the passage was a wall perpendicular to the curtain wall. This wall, about 0.8m wide, would only have been necessary if it supported another storey of the gatehouse which spanned the entire width of the structure. This room would have measured about 7.6m by 6.3m internally, giving the gatehouse a floor area of about 68.7m². While the gatehouse's internal measurements were larger than those of Peveril's keep (6.5m by 5.8m internally), the latter had an area of 75.4m² and far thicker walls, making it a far sturdier structure.

Archaeological evidence (see Chapter 3 below) suggests that Buckton was built sometime in the 12th or early-13th centuries, broadly at the same time as the earl of Chester built his castles at Bolingbroke, Chartley and Beeston (Fig 29). M. W. Thompson highlighted the similarity in design between Beeston, Bolingbroke, and Chartley castles, which are generally considered to have been built at the same time. The gatehouses and mural towers have walls 3m thick, are similar in size and shape, while the spacing between them and the width of the gate-passages vary little between the three castles. At Chartley, the presence of a previous timber castle with a motte influenced the design,[71] while at Beeston it is likely the earthworks of an Iron Age hillfort influenced the construction.[72] Bolingbroke Castle was built on a fresh site, meaning previous defences did not have to be taken into account.

Bolingbroke is a single enclosure laid out as a slightly irregular hexagon with a tower at five corners and a gatehouse with twin D-shaped towers in the northernmost corner. It is surrounded by a 30m wide moat.[73] A layer of made-up clay some 0.9 to 1.2m deep covers the

> **Archaeological evidence…suggests that Buckton was built sometime in the 12th or early 13th centuries, broadly at the same time as the earl of Chester built his castles at Bolingbroke, Chartley and Beeston**

site,[74] and one of the conclusions of excavations in the 1960s and 1970s was any stone buildings constructed on this layer would have required an undercroft. In the absence of any discovered undercrofts, it was concluded the buildings within the castle would have been primarily timber-framed throughout its history. Thompson remarked "The general appearance of Bolingbroke Castle at the time of its construction, with timber buildings clinging to its walls, may have resembled a great external shell keep, such as that at Berkley."[75] This may have been the arrangement at Buckton.

Fig 29: The innovative inner gatehouse at Beeston, with its D-shaped towers flanking the entrance passage. This was built in the 1220s.

Measured from the outer face of the curtain walls – which are 3.6m thick – the castle varies between about 58m and 67m wide;[76] and covers an area of approximately 2,500m^2.[77] The greater size meant towers could be added to the curtain wall. It is hardly surprising that Bolingbroke's moat was roughly three times wider than Buckton's; the natural slope surrounding Buckton made the approach difficult, whereas

Bolingbroke is a generally lowland area, sitting about 30m above sea level. Interestingly, both the interiors of Buckton and Bolingbroke were

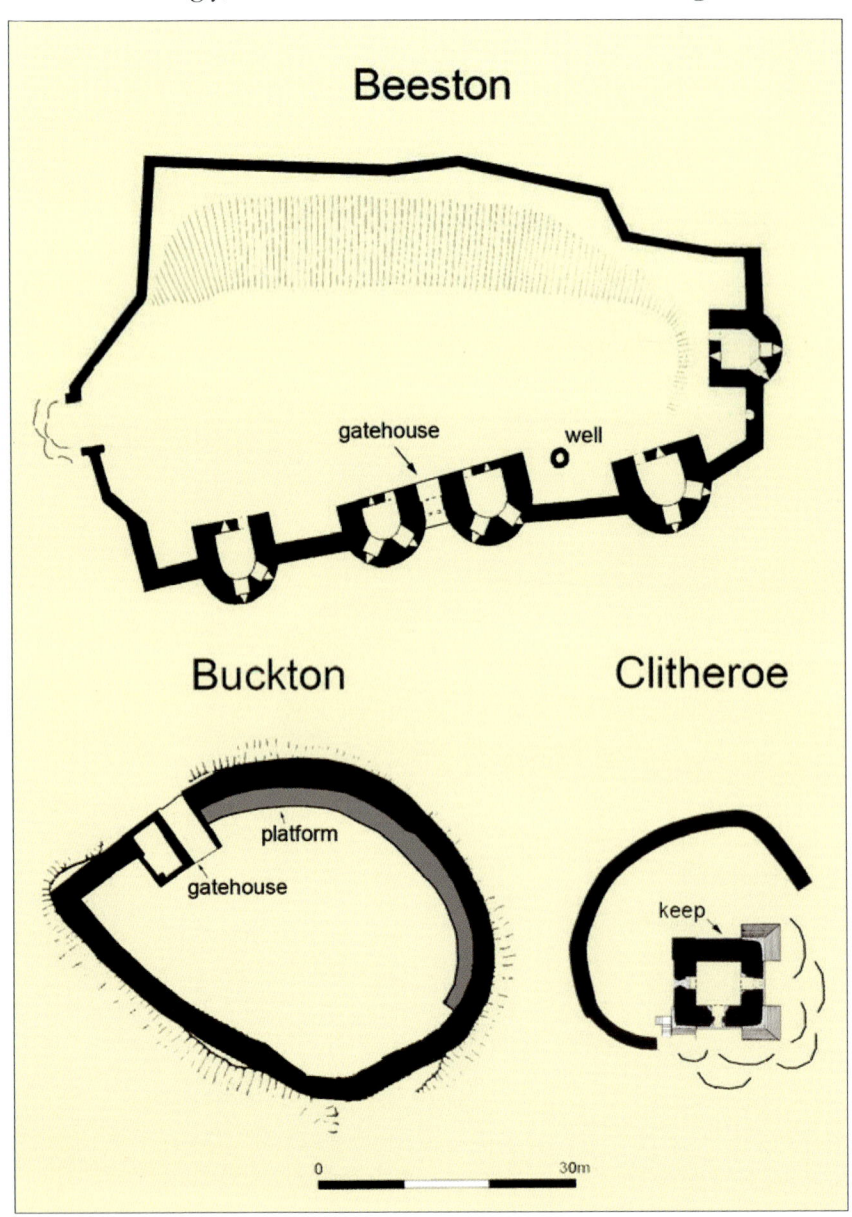

Fig 30: Comparative plans of Buckton Castle and the inner baileys at Beeston Castle and Clitheroe Castle.

> **Clitheroe's keep is the smallest in England...yet is still larger than Buckton's gatehouse**

raised above the natural level.

Unlike either Bolingbroke or Buckton, Beeston is divided into two closures. The inner enclosure occupies the highest point of the hill, while the outer enclosure is vast. Ellis points out this was most likely to encompass the earthworks of the Iron Age hillfort on the site, and denying them to any potential attackers.[78] The man-made defences do not encompass the whole of the outer enclosure, with walls built only around the east and south-east, as elsewhere the natural slope renders them redundant. The outer ward, with its curvilinear defences, measures up to 260m wide east to west, and between 150m and 190m north to south.[79] Even Beeston's inner enclosure dwarfs Buckton (Fig 30). It is an irregular polygon and measures between 31m and 47m north to south and 74m and 81m east to west. Interestingly the curtain walls of the inner enclosure at 2m thick are narrower than those at Buckton.[80]

Of the castles built by Ranulf de Blundeville, Chartley in Staffordshire bears the least similarity to Buckton.[81] Chartley has a motte which was surmounted by a stone keep some 10.7m in diameter internally with walls 3.7m thick.[82] As well as a motte, the castle has an inner and an outer bailey; the inner bailey measures 76m by 39m, and the outer is 60m by 55m.[83] Already in ruins by the 16th century, the curtain walls enclosing the castle are about 3.7m thick.[84]

What this demonstrates is that even in three diverse castles similarities can be found. Like Bolingbroke, Buckton's interior was raised. Though Thompson believes this means there could have been no stone buildings within the castle without an undercroft, this depends on the size of the structure and a small, stone building would not have needed deep foundations. While each of these four castles is stone-built, Buckton is the smallest, less than a third of the size of the next smallest (Bolingbroke). It is worth noting the castles built on fresh sites are also the smallest. But perhaps comparisons need to be sought further afield, beyond the property of the earls of Chester.

Elsewhere in the North West, the inner enclosure of Clitheroe Castle has some similarities with Buckton as discussed earlier (Fig 31). Externally, the footprint of the keep measures 10.4m square, excluding the buttresses at each corner.[85] It is unclear whether Clitheroe's keep is the smallest in England as Pettifer asserts,[86] or the second smallest surviving according to Lancashire County Archaeological Service.[87] Where it ranks should be discussed elsewhere, but it is certainly small and yet is

CHAPTER 2 The Political and Social Context of Buckton

still larger than Buckton's gatehouse which, including the passageway, measured 7.5m by 9.3m.

The small size of Clitheroe Castle has provoked comment and Hartley has suggested "The castle was built on the top of a limestone knoll in a good defensive position, perhaps negating the need for a substantial structure, although the poverty and isolation of Blackburn Hundred in the medieval period may have been the reason for the small size of the castle".[88] While Buckton is isolated from major centres of population, the earls of Chester to whom construction is usually attributed were wealthy magnates.

The Context of Buckton Castle

Castellarium Anglicanum, published in 1983, listed Buckton as an earthwork castle, specifically a ringwork.[89] By 1991 it was already known that

Fig 31: The late-12th century keep and curtain wall at Clitheroe Castle. This is a useful comparison for Buckton.

the castle had some stone walls,[90] which raises the issue of how many castles categorised as earthwork and timber had a stone phase. At Buckton, with little timber in the vicinity but an abundance of sandstone, the latter was naturally used as a building material.

A significant result of the excavation of Buckton Castle is the revision of its size. The estimate of 45m by 35m was based on the earthworks excluding the ditch. A more precise figure, courtesy of the excavations, is that the walls enclose 35.6m by 26.2m, reducing the area of the castle by 40 per cent. While earthworks may mark the outline of a site, it is important to consider that they may not represent the true extant of what lies beneath. At Buckton collapsing walls and slippage meant the earthworks were considerably wider than the actual wall.[91]

After the first season of excavations in 2008 it was felt that the "size, style, and construction method [of the curtain wall] implied a later medieval date and a castle of considerable status".[92] The curtain wall is indeed of a size comparable to the castles at Beeston and Bolingbroke, and larger than nearby Peveril's curtain wall, however, Buckton Castle is much smaller than the earl of Chester's other castles. Can such a small, isolated structure as Buckton really be "of considerable status"? The use of stone is somewhat deceptive because of environmental factors, and the increased cost of building in stone rather than timber means there is often a tendency to assume stone castles were inherently of higher status than their timber counterparts. While Buckton's high position meant it was visible for miles around, perhaps bringing in issues of symbolism, the size indicates that it was not a castle of the first rank. It was probably of lower status than either Bolingbroke or Beeston, although still of significance because it was one of the earliest stone-built castles in this part of the North West.

> **Buckton can no longer be considered a ringwork**

For much of the 20th century Buckton was classified as a ringwork castle; that is an oval or circular enclosure formed by the construction of earthen ramparts inside a ditch. After the latest excavations can Buckton still be considered a ringwork? With a ringwork, the earthen banks enclosing the site were a primary feature surmounted by either timber or masonry walls, in the same way that an earthen motte could have a tower built on top. We now know that at Buckton the banks accumulated over the stone walls after the castle was abandoned, therefore it can no longer be considered a ringwork. A possibility raised during the excavations was that it could be a shell keep.[93] The National

Monuments Record Monument Type thesaurus describes a shell keep as "a Norman keep, in the form of a circular or polygonal enclosure surrounded by a wall".[94] One of the best preserved shell keeps in England is Restormel in Cornwall. The circular shell keep replaced timber defences in the 13th century and its walls are 2.4m thick and 7.9m tall and crested by a wall walk.[95] Measuring from the outer face it is 39m in diameter.[96] Durham in County Durham, Farnham in Surrey, Pickering in Yorkshire, and Windsor in Berkshire are all examples of shell keeps.[97] Common between these examples is that their outlines were either circular or near circular. Buckton does not fit within this pattern, and while that on its own might not exclude it from this categorisation,

Fig 32: An aerial view of the landscape context of Buckton Castle, showing the heather moorland to the right and the Micklehurst Brook to the left.

the lack of evidence of structures built against the curtain wall is more suggestive. While it is possible Buckton was never finished (see Chapter 3) – which may explain why no internal buildings have been found – the evidence points towards it not being a shell keep.

Brown has noted "the historian's habit of trying to make a tidy pattern out of the untidy past" can sometimes be problematic.[98] While it can aid analysis, being too concerned with pigeon-holing a structure can be detrimental to understanding it. Although there are still many uncertainties surrounding Buckton Castle (Fig 32), there are some categories we can apply to it. It is a small, highland, rural, masonry castle. What this should show is that Buckton Castle is unusual, a reminder that within the more than 1,500 castles in England a great deal of variety exists. Instead it seems reasonable to classify Buckton as an enclosure castle "a defended residence or stronghold, built mainly of stone, in which the principal or sole defence comprises the walls and towers bounding the site".[99]

While Buckton is a small site, and it is difficult to imagine it containing luxurious accommodation, the prominence of the site may be important. As noted earlier, highland sites such as Buckton and Beeston are uncommon in England and display may have been a factor in choosing the site. It would surely have been a prominent symbol of the earl's lordship. The issue of display may be particularly important because it was at the extremity of the earl's holdings. Castle gatehouses have been a focus for display, often displaying the coats of arms of the owners and being visually impressive.[100] Using the entrance to the castle as a focus of display emphasises the importance of entering the owner's building. Similar issues may have been in play with Buckton; while it may not have been situated along a major thoroughfare it would have stood out at the edge of the earl of Chester's landholding as a territorial marker, making it known that people were entering the County Palatine of Chester.

Excavation and Survey at Buckton Castle CHAPTER 3

Fig 33: The Buckton Castle excavations in 2010. Picture courtesy of Suave Aerial Photographers.

Chapter 3

Excavation and Survey at Buckton Castle

Introduction

Buckton Castle has attracted the interest of antiquarians and treasure hunters

Buckton Castle has attracted the interest of antiquarians and treasure hunters since the 18th century, though the first archaeological investigations were not carried out until the 1990s. Between 1996 and 2002 the University of Manchester Archaeological Unit (UMAU) conducted landscape survey, small-scale excavations, and remedial work, the latter repairing damage caused by unauthorised digging of the Scheduled Ancient Monument.[1] A larger investigation programme was undertaken during the 2000s (Fig 33), commissioned by Tameside Metropolitan Borough Council and completed by the University of Salford. Three seasons of excavations between 2007 and 2010 (Fig 34) were designed to assess the date, phasing, and extent of the surviving archaeological

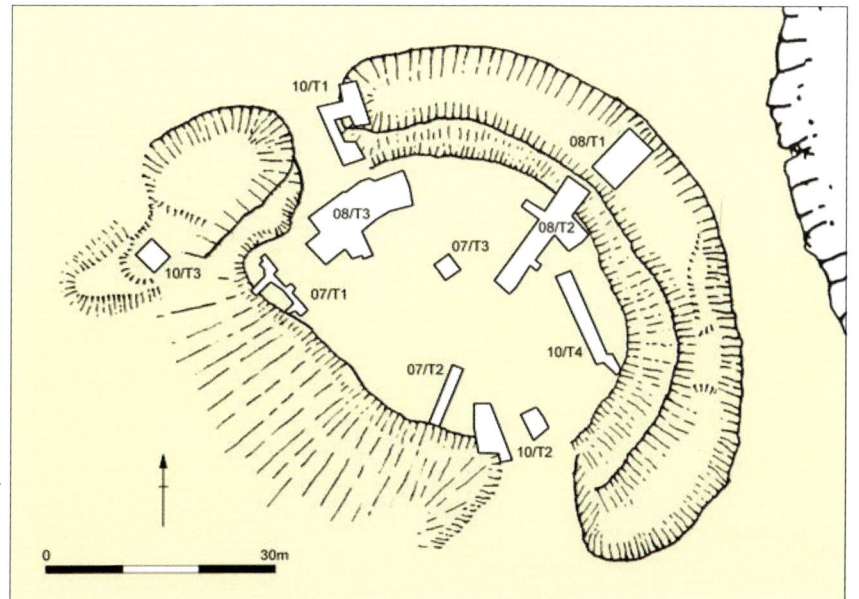

Fig 34: The location of the trenches excavated at Buckton Castle between 2007 and 2010

remains comprising the monument[2] with a significant community element intended to widen local participation in the project and provide training for local archaeology volunteers.

The fieldwork undertaken in 1996 and 1998 (Fig 35 & Fig 37) focussed upon accurately recording the surviving earthworks of the castle and investigation of an area to the north of the main earthworks through excavation. The earthwork survey showed that the absence of a ditch on the western side of the monument was due to the steepness of the slope rendering its presence redundant. The excavations in 1996 on the putative outer bailey to the north of the monument (Fig 37) demonstrated a pair of curving banks was of recent origin, probably connected to earth moving activities associated with the nearby quarry during the 1950s. If any earlier archaeological features were present in this area, such as the approach road to the northern entrance of the castle, they had been at best heavily disturbed and at worst removed by this activity.

Damage to the interior of the monument in 1999 and again in 2002 due to illegal digging led to the excavation of a series of test pits within the damaged areas (Fig 35). These revealed details about the pre-castle

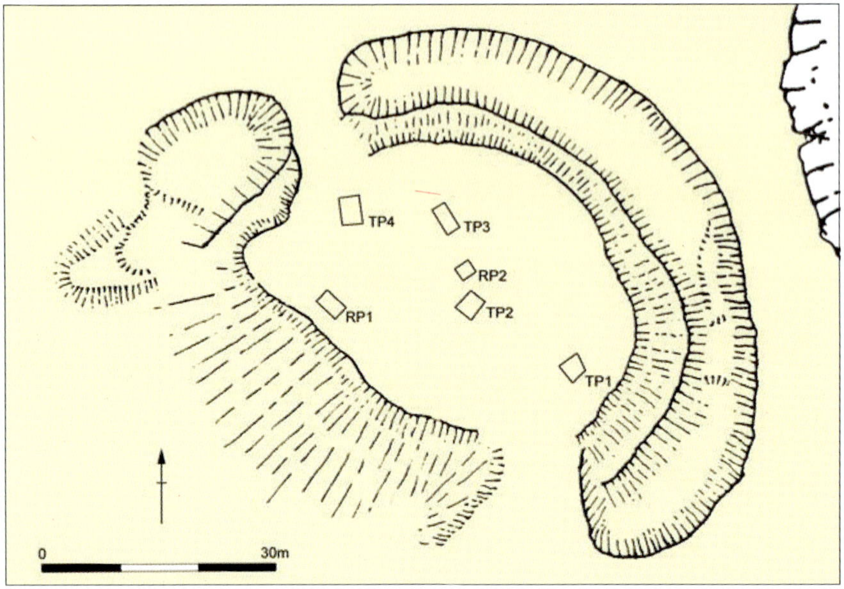

The fieldwork undertaken during the 1990s focussed upon accurately recording the surviving earthworks of the castle

Fig 35: The location of the 1998 test pits (TP) and the 2002 robber pits (RP).

CHAPTER 3 Excavation and Survey at Buckton Castle

Fig 36: The heather moorland and blanket peat landscape around Buckton has remained largely unchanged for hundreds of years.

landscape, in the form of buried land surfaces sealed by peat layers, and the make-up of the castle platform.

The 2007 to 2010 excavations were focussed on defining the extant of the castle remains, examining the ditch, banks, curtain wall, parts of the interior and the northern and southern entrances. A key element of this programme was the excavation of several sections of the ditch with the intention of locating datable artefacts and palaeo-environmental deposits that would throw light upon the phasing of the monument and development of the landscape around the castle (Fig 36).

The Pre-Castle Landscape

The present landscape around the castle is dominated by the Pennine escarpment immediately west of the monument, heather moorland and blanket peat to the north and north-east of the site, and Buckton Quarry that abuts the eastern side of the earthworks. Late 20th century research into the environmental history of the southern Pennine uplands has indicated that the blanket peat deposits and moorland originated between 5500 and 3000BC.[3] Buckton was thus established on an escarpment dominated by peat and heather moorland.

Precisely what the immediate pre-castle landscape looked like was revealed in deposits from beneath the castle in two test pits excavated in 1998 (Fig 35). Test Pit 1998/2 was dug into an old robber pit in the middle of the monument's interior and Test Pit 1998/3 was dug south-east of the northern entrance.

Both test pits produced gritstone make-up levels, 0.4m and 1m deep respectively; each sealed a peat layer 0.05m and 0.2m deep respectively. Palaeo-environmental samples were taken from the peat layers in both test pits. The two samples taken from Test Pit 1998/3 (Fig 35) were from the top (sample TP2) and bottom (sample TP2n) of the peat layer, whilst a bulk sample was taken from the thinner deposits in Test Pit 3. Each sample was radio-carbon dated.

All three samples were dominated by heathland pollen types (heather and bilberry), with the pollen for birch, oak, and willow showing a decline between the lower sample TP2n and higher sample TP2, hinting at deforestation close by.[4] Furthermore, the presence of pollen from five weed species in the Test Pit 2 samples (*Asteraceae*, *Artemisia*, *Plantago*, *Rumex*, and *Umbelliferae*) indicated more localised disturbance of the ground surface. The pollen analysis from both test pits indicated a change from a mixed heath-scrub landscape to a relatively open heathland landscape.

The radio-carbon dates obtained suggested TP3 was the oldest of the samples, being dated to the period Cal AD 570-765, whilst TP2 and TP2n were of broadly similar date being dated to the periods Cal AD 765 to 1010 and Cal AD 700 to 1000 respectively.[5] It seems likely these peat layers can be interpreted as deposits that were truncated as part of the clearance activity undertaken across the castle site before the construction of the ditch and the raising of the inner platform was begun.

The excavation of these six robber pits revealed deposits relating to the pre-castle landscape in three of the pits

Fig 37: Trench 2, excavated in 1996, revealed the pre-castle land surface (orange weathered stone) to the north of the castle. It also revealed the western bank (the black hump in the trench section to the left) identified in 1991 as a possible outer bailey. This turned out to be a mid-20th century landscaping feature.

Pollen analysis from both test pits indicated a change from a mixed heath-scrub landscape to a relatively open heathland landscape

Whatever the date of this construction activity, which is discussed at the end of the current chapter, it cannot have taken place before the 11th century.

Fig 38: Trench 2010/1 showing the ditch terminus (left) and the causeway (right). Picture courtesy of Suave Aerial Photographers.

The Ditch

Buckton Castle's ditch system was investigated for the first time in 2008.[6] Trench 2008/1, located across the eastern ditch, provided evidence for the nature of the composition of the inner mound and the phases of subsequent abandonment and deterioration of the masonry from the outer mural defences into the rock-cut ditch. Unfortunately, no reliable dating evidence was recovered from these archaeological deposits. However, the excavation of this feature did provide irrefutable evidence for the primary phases of the construction of the monument, with evidence to show that it was first and foremost a stone-built structure. After the initial cutting of the ditch there was a period of ero-

After the initial cutting of the ditch there was a period of erosion mostly from the looser deposits of the inner raised platform

sion mostly from the looser deposits of the inner raised platform. Then the ditch appears to have been partially re-cut before being filled with rubble masonry from the curtain wall.

Trench 2010/1 (Fig 38) was opened over the northern earthworks associated with the entrance causeway and ditch.[7] The trench was sited to confirm the depth of the original ditch and its relationship to the causeway and to produce a profile in section of this relationship. It was also intended to ascertain the nature and composition of the fabric used on the causeway, the method of its construction, and the possibility of the presence of any associated structures. The trench was roughly H-shaped with two north-south orientated sections – one along the causeway and the other across the ditch – linked by an east-west section extending up the slope of the causeway. A wide sondage was cut along the length of the causeway section of the trench (Slot A) to ascertain the depth of any demolition layers, and the presence of any underlying features (Fig 39). The demolition layers comprised large fragments of sandstone rubble and ashlar blocks from the outer face of the northern curtain wall. Several small post- and stake-holes were discovered in the

Fig 39: Trench 2010/1 showed the same sequence of fills as trench 2008/1.

CHAPTER 3 Excavation and Survey at Buckton Castle

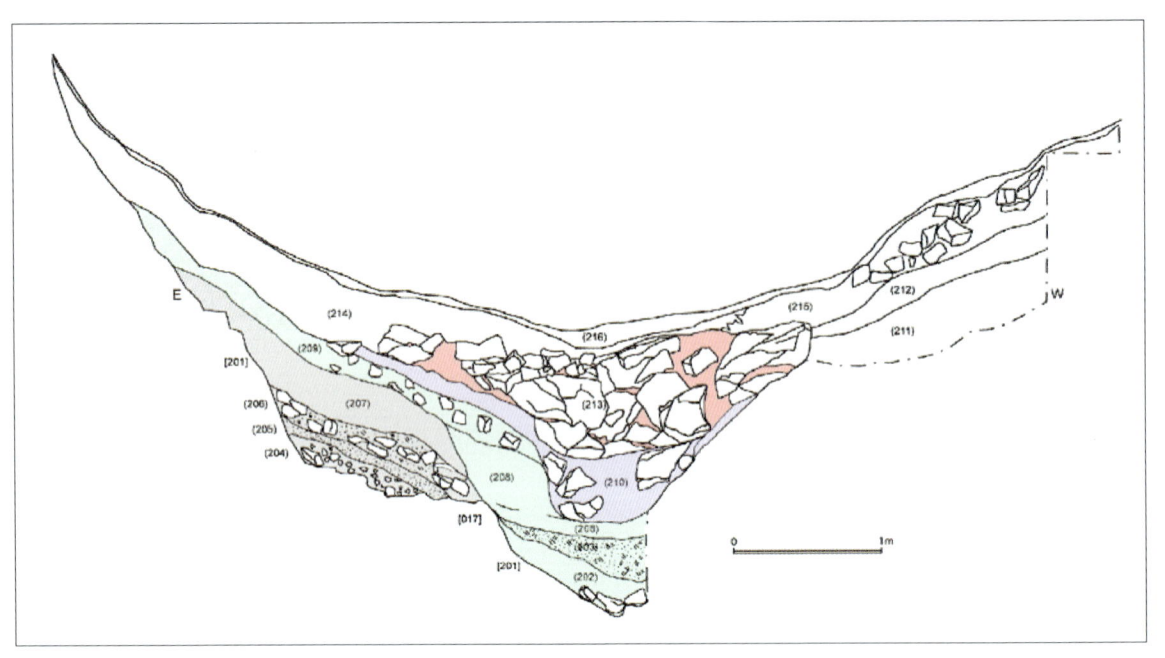

Fig 40: The eastern castle ditch in Trench 2008/1 shows evidence for three major phases of activity. Key: grey - undisturbed natural; green - primary ditch fill; lilac - second re-cut and fill; red - rubble deposit from the curtain wall.

east facing section of this sondage but were not visible in plan during excavation. The lower section of Trench 2010/1 was excavated to ascertain the stratigraphic profile and full depth of the ditch and to confirm the presence or absence of a terminus. The ditch was discovered to be rock-cut, as in trench 2008/1 (Fig 40), with a rounded terminus. The narrow east-west strip leading up the causeway slope was intended to uncover the construction of the causeway and revealed it to be of natural bedrock into which the ditch had been cut on both sides.

Trench 2010/1 produced significant information on the construction, use and demise of Buckton Castle. Evidence was uncovered to suggest three possible phases of distinct activity: firstly a primary phase associated with the original excavation of the ditch and construction of the monument; secondly, cleaning and occupation activity; and finally its abandonment or destruction.

The first phase of activity covered the original excavation and cutting of the ditch, and was contemporary with the construction of the inner mound. The same material excavated from the ditch was used to raise the level of the interior of the castle by at least 1m across the site. After the original cutting of the ditch primary sediments filled the bottom of the ditch. This was visible as erosion and slumping into the ditch from deposits to the north and south of the feature. Clearly these deposits were accumulating naturally and sporadically and their build-up would suggest there was no active maintenance of the ditch during this time. Although the time span is unclear the shallowness of these deposits suggests years rather than decades. This early phase of activity was also seen on the causeway where a rough metalled surface was laid. Cut into this layer were the post- and stake-holes found in Slot A. These might be associated with the construction of associated gate structures, as identified in the 2008 excavations (see below) or evidence of randomly placed posts along the causeway.

> **The ditch appears to have been partially re-cut before being filled with rubble masonry**

The second phase of activity was a re-cut of the ditch, represented by a narrower V-shaped cut achieving the same depth as the original excavation. The evidence for the re-cutting of the ditch was clear from the nature of the fills with the lower appearing more homogenous, primarily comprising clayey-silts or degraded sands with small fragments of naturally occurring laminated sandstone indicative of gradual and intermittent natural deposition of deposits into the ditch.

The third phase of activity in Trench 2010/1 was represented the final collapse of the revetment wall and gatehouse structure in to the ditch and over the causeway as a rubble infill and spread, and the subsequent accumulation of peaty soils over the upper rubble fill of the ditch. It is impossible to say at what date this collapse/demolition occurred, although the discovery of 19th and 20th century artefacts in the upper rubble levels of eastern ditch section during the 2008 excavations, and the presence of robber activity across the site, would suggest that erosion of the monument continued throughout the post-medieval period.

The Curtain Wall

One of the aims of the 2007-2010 excavation programme was to investigate the banks of the castle in order to determine whether the Buckton was an earthwork or a stone structure. Hints of stonework surviving within the castle had already been suggested by two sources. Firstly a 16th century estate map that appears to show a wall on top of the bank. Secondly, the unlicensed digging had revealed in 1981 and 2002 an ashlar-faced stone wall in the north-western corner of the bank.[8]

The presence of stone structures raised questions about the form of the castle, not least its classification as an earthen ringwork.

Trench 2007/1 was opened over the western castle earthworks.[9] At the apex of the embankment a masonry wall was discovered a few centimetres below the vegetation and soil cover. On further investigation this was found to be 2.8m wide and excavated to a depth of *c.* 1.6m. It was made up of an inner and outer course of ashlar containing a rubble and lime mortar fill. Trench 2007/2 (Fig 41) in the north-western corner of the earthworks, on the site of the 1981 and 2002 illegal digging work, showed the wall extended into this area, the inner ashlar face forming a right angle before carrying on eastwards to form a wall along the northern bank. In both trenches the foundations of the walls rested on solid rock, whilst the inner, eastern face of the walls had rubble deposits abutting the wall indicating the upper deposits of the raised platform was constructed later. No artefactual dating evidence came from

This trench provided evidence for at least two phases of construction

Fig 41: The masonry discovered in the robber pits of 1981 and 2002 was excavated in Trench 2007/2, and was found to form part of the north-western corner of the curtain wall.

Fig 42: The enigmatic stone platform behind the curtain wall in Trench 2008/2. It overlies part of the curtain wall which appears to have collapsed (centre left of the picture).

either of these trenches.

Trench 2008/2 (Fig 42) was located over the eastern embankment and was positioned to assess whether the curtain wall seen on the western side of the castle in 2007 extended around the eastern circuit of the defences.[10] This trench provided evidence for at least two phases of construction during the life-span of the castle. There was an initial phase of fortification that saw the erection of a stone curtain wall, *c.* 2.8m wide with ashlar facings, broadly contemporary with the excavation of the outer ditch and the raising of the inner mound. A second phase of construction necessitated the modification of the extant defences (a section of which had collapsed) and the construction of an internal stone platform, *c.* 0.45m deep and c. 1.8m wide, with an ashlar kerb, following the inside circumference of the eastern curtain wall. This stone platform abutted the inner edge of the eastern curtain wall in several places, and in Trench 2008/2 even overlay a small collapsed section of inner face of the curtain wall. The purpose of this platform is uncertain; it may have been the foundation for a series of internal buildings abutting the curtain wall or it may have been used as some form of walkway. There is little indication how soon it was built after the curtain wall, although the fact that it overlay a small collapsed section of the inner face of the curtain wall suggests that this gap was more likely to be years than months.

The results from Trench 2008/2 also corroborated and supported the evidence from Trenches 2007/1 and 2007/2 for the way in which the curtain wall had been built. There was no foundation cut present, the foundations being sited below the level of the upcast sandstone levelling layer. This confirmed that the wall foundations were already in place when the levelling material was upcast onto the mound, indicating that the primary phase of construction at Buckton comprised a stone-built curtain wall, as opposed to an earthen bank and timber palisade.

Trench 2010/2 was opened over the earthworks along the southern edge of the castle to investigate the southern entrance into Buckton.[11] This feature was believed to be part of a farm track, first recorded on maps from the 19th century. The trench was split into two, with sections exposing the curtain wall on both sides of the trackway. The main trench to the north-west of the opening was designed to assess the construction of the wall and the damage caused by the 19th century truncation. A series of sondages were excavated on both sides of the wall to reveal its depth and any foundations present. Slot B was excavated on the north-eastern, inner, side of the curtain wall and cut through the interior surface of the castle to investigate the nature of any foundations underlying the internal facing. Slot C was excavated alongside the south-western face of the curtain wall to expose any external foundations. The wall foundations were found to survive across the trench and beneath the truncation of the 19th century trackway.

Trench 2010/2 (Fig 43) exposed a large section of the curtain wall revealing the full height of the structure in the early 21st century. Despite its truncation during the 19th century the wall was found to be in a reasonable condition and standing at over 1.5m high in some places. This trench was able to give a profile showing the construction of the

Trench 2010/2 exposed a large section of the curtain wall

Fig 43: The best-preserved stretch of curtain wall was excavated at the southern end of the castle in Trench 2010/2, where it stood more than 1m high.

inner mound. An extension of the trench, Trench 2010/2a, was opened to the south-east of the trackway. This extension was designed to ascertain whether the continuation of the curtain wall to the south was constructed in a curved or angled alignment. The trench followed the contours of the rampart to reveal considerable erosion at the south-western end of the exposed wall length, which was uncovered to its lowest facing course. Despite this disturbance a curve could be identified in the exposed curtain wall.

This trench also provided the evidence for the primary construction sequence of the castle. In Slot B the wall foundation was found to lie over a grey, granular, degraded stone deposit, also seen in Trench 2010/1, lying on top of the sandy natural bedrock. Elsewhere this degraded stone deposit is sealed by a thin layer of peat at varying thicknesses (0.05m-0.4m) and appears to represent the pre-castle landscape surface (see above). The construction of the curtain wall represents the next phase of activity in Trench 2010/2. During excavations no foundations were identified to support the wall and there is no evidence of a cut in the underlying deposit. This potential structural problem seems to have been mitigated by both the raising of the castle interior and the deposition of the external up-cast layers. This levelling activity covered the lower courses of the wall on both sides to a depth of 1.5m on the interior and 0.5m on the exterior faces. It is unclear whether these external deposits were contemporary with the curtain wall or were laid down later as additional support against erosion into the ditch. The final phase seen in this trench was associated with the decline of the castle and its defences. As seen in Trench 2010/1 the curtain wall was subject to demolition/collapse. Unlike Trench 2010/1, the curtain wall in this area was subject to further disturbance by its truncation sometime in the 19th century. The cutting of the wall and removal of both ashlar courses can clearly be seen as a stepped profile in both Trench 2010/2 and 2a. The wide V-shaped cut was found to be deeper than the wall itself with the lower part filled by re-deposited rubble from the wall's core which had eroded over the course of the past century. The lack of dressed blocks in this fill can be attributed to robber activity across the monument.

The Gatehouse

The chief aim of the 2008 season was to investigate the northern entrance of the castle. Test Pit 4 in 1998 had demonstrated this area had been heavily disturbed by late 18th and 19th century excavation activity so it was unclear what stratified remains might survive.[12]

Despite this earlier activity enough in-situ structural evidence remained in Trench 2008/3 (Figs 44 & 48) to indicate the presence of a gatehouse. The ground floor comprised a western rectangular room, a guardroom perhaps,[13] 3.3m by 6.3m internally, with walls standing in places more than 1m high. To the east was a gate-passage 3.3m wide. All the walls of the possible guardroom were consistently faced with ashlar blocks of sandstone fronting a sandstone rubble core, which has been inadvertently exposed through robber activity on partial sections of the eastern elevation of wall in Slot H. The northern extent of the gatehouse structure was 'embedded'/incorporated into the external

The chief aim of the 2008 season was to investigate the northern entrance of the castle

northern curtain wall, running east-west in this area of the site, with the northern wall butting the outer rampart at this point, and the western wall keyed into the curtain wall,[14] indicating this could have formed part of the primary phase of mural defences, rather than being a secondary phase of modification. The north-western corner of the gatehouse projected beyond the perimeter of this mural defence, onto the causeway; although the north-eastern corner was flush with the outer face of the curtain wall.

The quantity of rubble in-fill excavated in 2008[15] suggested the gatehouse structure could have been at least two-storeys high, and possibly extended across the gate-passage to the east, as similar rubble and debris deposits were identified in a section through the overburden in this area.[16]

Fig 44: The gatehouse during excavation in 2008 in Trench 2008/3.

A possible phase break in the northern section of eastern wall of the gatehouse hinted at multiple phases of construction, with the suggestion of a blocked entrance leading from the gatepassage[17] into the north-east corner of the gatehouse itself visible in the west-facing elevation of eastern wall. An enigmatic row of kerb stones running east-west and embedded into the secondary metalled surface of the gate-passage appeared to project under the eastern wall in conjunction with the possible break in phasing. This kerb appeared to demarcate the boundary between two different metalled surfaces in the entrance and could have been associated with a portcullis or gate, which would have ultimately closed the entrance. This feature was mirrored by the presence of a post-hole in the overlying metalled surface, centrally positioned within the entrance way (Fig 45). This was possibly related to the modification

Fig 45: The metalling in the gatepassage during excavation in 2008.

Fig 46: The eastern wall of the gate-passage was found, in 2008, to survive up to a height of 1m in Trench 2008/3.

of the entrance area, and was suggestive of scaffolding for a wooden forma to support the construction of an arched gateway. The truncation of the uppermost metalled surface by this feature would suggest this may have been one of the last phases of construction/modification activity associated with the castle. No datable material was excavated from this feature.

Overlying the surfaces and post-hole was a spread of burnt material, principally clay and silt, which provided the only datable artefactual material to date, contemporary with the construction of the monument. This layer[19] produced the only habitation waste in the form of datable ceramic evidence, butchered animal bone including rib and legs bones of sheep, and charcoal indicative of occupation debris. This layer may have been part of a structural collapse of the rooms above the gate-passage, again supporting the idea of a two-storey building over the entrance. The clay was partially scorched in patches, though there was neither evidence for structural timbers associated with this collapse nor an intense heat, which would have vitrified parts of the surface.

Above these sealed deposits, several episodes of rubble collapse, possibly as a result of the natural decay of the structural remains, and subsequent re-deposition of material as a consequence of illicit excavations, created a build-up of demolition rubble. This was sealed by the modern ground surface of peat and soil.

To the east of the entrance, the opposing wall for the gate-passage remained partially intact (Fig 46), approximately 3.3m to the east of the

Fig 47: The collapsed northern wall of the gate-house (left) was excavated in Trench 2010/2. Picture courtesy of Suave Aerial Photographers.

eastern gatehouse wall. This wall served to 'square-off' the curtain wall. The weight of these walls against the eastern wall of the entrance has forced its near collapse, resulting in an arched profile, mirrored by the partially collapsed section of the eastern gatehouse wall. The inner face of the curtain wall to the east of the entrance has suffered heavily from later disturbance and only a *c.* 2.5m section of the ashlar (roughly dressed) facing stones survives to indicate its southern elevation.

Though no decorative masonry or dressed architectural stonework was found, archaeological deposits associated with the later phases of floor surfaces in the gate-passage provided dating evidence in the form of artefactual material (Fig 52); fragments from at least two ceramic vessels, datable to the late-11th to 13th centuries, associated with organic debris (scraps of burnt bone and leather) and residual charcoal; tantalising evidence for the occupation of the castle during this period.

Fig 48: The excavated plan of the gatehouse in 2008.

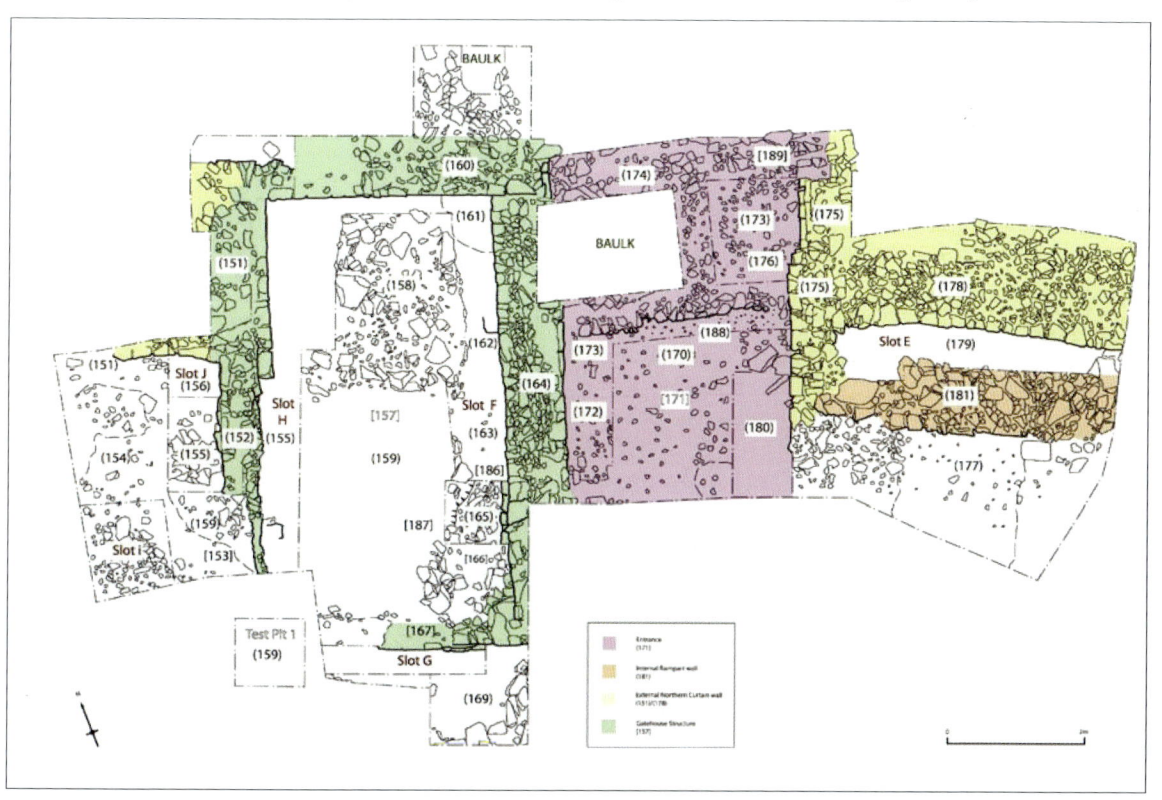

In the following season Trench 2010/2 examined the causeway leading to the northern entrance.[20] This provided evidence for the final phase of the gatehouse. Rubble layers containing ashlar blocks excavated on top of the causeway, close to the entrance, were interpreted as evidence of the collapse, or perhaps demolition, of the gatehouse. However, it was impossible to say when this collapse occurred, other than it appears to have taken place before the post-medieval records of the site began in the 16th century.

The Interior

The investigation of the interior of Buckton Castle was made problematic by the disturbance resulting from prolonged treasure hunting and robbing activities. The extensive nature of this disturbance was revealed by earthwork and aerial surveys during the mid-1990s.[21] Whilst these showed the treasure and robber pits extended all over the interior of the castle, the western half of the monument was more damaged than the eastern half, being almost completely covered in pits.

In order to assess the damage to the western side of the monument by this earlier treasure hunting and quarrying activity a scheme was devised to re-excavate some of the old pits. With Scheduled Ancient Monument Consent having been granted, in July 1998 four of the pits were excavated. The pits were excavated to the solid geology, the sections cleaned, and samples taken for palaeo-environmental analysis and radio-carbon dating. When in June 2002 two pits were illegally dug into the western half of the castle, presumably by treasure hunters, Scheduled Ancient Monument Consent was again obtained and the pits cleaned and recorded in the same manner as the work undertaken during 1998. Neither were excavated to the solid geology.[22]

The excavation of these six robber pits revealed deposits relating to the pre-castle landscape in three of the pits (see above). Test Pit 1998/1 lay immediately north of the southern entrance and Trench 2010/2. Test Pit 1998/2 lay close to the middle of the western embankment, whilst Test Pit 1998/3 9Fig 37) lay to the south-east of the northern entrance. Finally, Test Pit 1998/4 lay immediately west of the northern gateway and Trench 2010/1 and was found to be full of stone rubble deposits. All four test pits produced evidence of a yellow-brown and orange-brown gritstone make-up levels ranging from 0.2m to 1m thick.

Rubble layers...excavated on top of the causeway, close to the entrance, were interpreted as evidence of the collapse, or perhaps demolition, of the gatehouse

In two of the test pits (1998/2 and 1998/3) these make-up levels sealed a charcoal and peat layer, which represented the pre-castle surface (see above). Test Pit 1998/3 also revealed a stone structure, running east to west for roughly 1.1m. This feature took the form of a line of eleven gritstone blocks sitting on top of the orange brown gritstone layer. There was a dark loamy area on either side of the 'wall' alignment. This structure might possibly represent the truncated remains of a 'dwarf wall' on which upright timbers could have been set.

Robber Pit 2 from 2002 was 0.75m by 0.5m in plan. It was cut into an earlier pit to a depth of 1.1m revealing a yellow-brown and below this an orange gritstone make-up level, as noted in the 1998 test pits. Robber Pit 1 from 2002 was 1.2m by 0.7m in plan and was found to be a re-cut of an earlier robber pit, first noticed in 1981. It was located in the north-western corner of the monument and produced evidence in the western face of the pit for an ashlar-faced stone wall cut into the banking to a depth of 1m. The eastern pit section contained similar make-up deposits to those seen in Robber Pit 2. The location of the ashlar wall

Fig 49: The eastern curtain wall and interior deposits as excavated in Trench 2008/2. The platform (purple) can be seen to overlie part of the curtain wall (orange)

Fig 50: The eastern curtain wall and interior deposits as excavated in Trench 2010/4. Picture courtesy of Suave Aerial Photographers.

in this pit led to the designing of the research-driven fieldwork that became the three seasons of work undertaken between 2007 and 2010.

The programme of work from 2007 to 2010 allowed the targeting of hitherto uninvestigated parts of the interior in a manner decided by the research strategy of the archaeologists, rather than the treasure hunters. Trench 2007/3 was opened in the middle of the castle to the west of the Test Pit 1998/3, which had produced the evidence for a probable dwarf wall.[23] Only deposits associated with the gritstone make-up level of the castle were located.

Trench 2008/2 (Fig 49), on the eastern side of the interior, investigated the approximate location of a ruined building shown on a map made in 1842 by the Saddleworth Geological Society.[24] This trench, whose eastern end encountered the curtain wall, failed to locate any structural remains relating to this building, instead coming down on to the top of the gritstone make-up level seen elsewhere within the interior. This was confirmed in Slot A which was dug to a depth of 0.5m into this make-up level.

Trench 2010/4 (Fig 50) was opened behind and parallel to the eastern curtain wall in a further attempt to locate the ruined building recorded in 1842.[25] At its southern end the trench encountered the curtain wall. The northern and central areas of the trench revealed levelling layers of stone chippings of varying sizes, unlike the gritstone make-up levels seen elsewhere. These possibly related to floor surfaces, although whether internal or external was unclear. A sondage (Slot E) was excavated on the western side of the trench to ascertain the depth of these potential floors and investigate the possibility of structural remains at a lower level. It uncovered a post-hole and linear feature at this lower level, although there was no indication of any other structural remains. Beneath these deposits was the top of the gritstone make-up level of the castle.

Five seasons of work within the interior of the castle (1998, 2002, 2007, 2008, and 2010) failed to uncover any artefactual evidence. However, there was some evidence in two separate areas (Test Pit 1998/3 and Trench 2010/4) for occupation activity, one of which was associated with a probable wall alignment.

The Form and Phasing of Buckton Castle

As discussed in the previous chapter, Buckton Castle can no longer be considered a ringwork, but may be more accurately described as an enclosure castle. Evidence from the 2007, 2008, and 2010 excavations points to three main phases of activity (Fig 51). Firstly, the initial castle building phase which saw digging of the ditch creating the northern causeway, the raising of the inner platform by *c*. 1m and the construction of the curtain wall and gatehouse. The second phase saw the re-cutting of the castle ditch and the addition of the platform to the rear of the eastern curtain wall. The final major period of activity on the site saw the abandonment of the castle, which led to the rapid collapse of the eastern curtain wall and gatehouse. The nature of the rubble deposits within the sections of ditch excavated (on the eastern side of the castle and adjacent to the causeway) strongly suggest a single deposition act of partial demolition, possibly to be interpreted as slighting, followed by a long period of rubble accumulation through neglect. Later activity included the cutting of an access way through the southern curtain wall, the robbing of the curtain wall in other places, and the digging of pits in the interior of the castle.

Throughout investigations in the 1990s and during the period 2007-10 there was a paucity of datable artefactual evidence from well-stratified (sealed) archaeological deposits on site. However, during the 2008 excavations an uncontaminated deposit associated with the uppermost metalled surface of the northern entrance way was revealed. Ceramic evidence (Fig 52) and possible occupation debris, including charcoal and burnt bone (Fig 53) were recovered from this context, which was found below demolition deposits associated with the collapse of the structural remains of the entrance. It is possible this isolated group of material, comprising two ceramic vessels datable to the late-12th cen-

Fig 51: the excavated features at Buckton Castle, 2007 to 2010. showing the curtain wall and gatehouse.

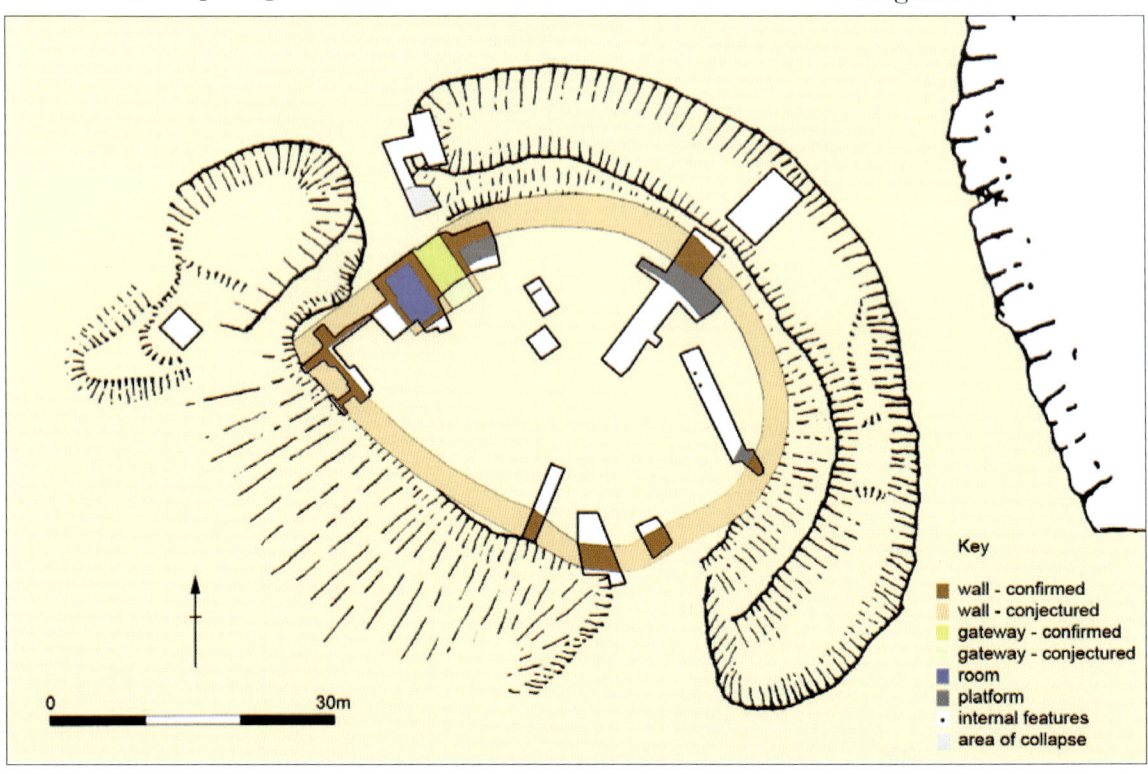

Fig 52: Right: the four sherds of Pennine Gritty ware excavated from the gate-passage in 2008.

Fig 53: Far right: the butchered animal bone excavated from the gate-passage deposits in 2008.

Evidence from the 2007, 2008, and 2010 excavations points to three main phases of activity

tury as Pennine Gritty Ware, were deposited during the first two construction phases, prior to the active decommissioning or passive abandonment of the monument.[26]

One interpretation of this structural and phasing evidence is that Buckton Castle was short-lived. The evidence for this is the lack, so far, of any architectural stone work uncovered during the excavations of 2007, 2008, and 2010. This suggests the castle was never finished, at least to a high standard with the typical architectural dressed features of the Norman period. Also, only minimal quantities of contemporary medieval pottery were unearthed. Given such a lack of artefactual/occupation material conclusions about the phasing of the site have to be drawn largely from stratigraphic and architectural evidence. The ditch section excavated in Trench 2010/1 revealed possible multiphase activity with a period of natural infilling followed by a re-cutting finally ending with the collapse of the wall and gatehouse. Whilst it has been suggested the castle was never completed the evidence of re-cutting of the ditch would suggest a longer-term occupation. However, when reviewing the historical evidence suggested for the builder of the castle (see below) the episode of re-cutting could equally be interpreted as returning to the castle during times of stress when the Earl of Chester was in dispute with King Stephen and/or King David of Scotland after more settled periods when the castle was not in use or construction had

CHAPTER 3 Excavation and Survey at Buckton Castle

81

been suspended.

Had Trench 2010/3 provided evidence of an outwork it might have offered a position from which the garrison would have been able to provide enfilading fire on anyone approaching the gateway. However, no evidence of masonry or other material was found in this trench. It was evident the mound consisted of a deep layer (over 0.75m) of crushed yellow sandstone and large angular inclusions very similar to the make-up layer found on the interior of the castle that has been interpreted as a levelling layer formed from the up cast material from the ditch construction. Perhaps this feature was a spoil-heap from the primary castle construction or the cleaning of the ditch in the second phase of activity?

An important issue arising from the excavations is whether Buckton Castle was ever completed. The lack of decorative masonry or dressed architectural stonework around the gatehouse, combined with the paucity of artefactual evidence suggests that habitation was short-lived and construction may have been aborted. The purpose of the platform behind the eastern curtain wall and the relationship between the two raises further questions. Why was the platform not found behind the western wall? Is it significant that the western side of the castle was too steep to be approached? Aside from this platform, the only finished floor discovered within the castle was in the gatehouse. There is the possibility that the platform may have acted as a foundation for timber buildings intended to be built against the inner face of the curtain wall, or it may simply have been a walkway. As speculated in Chapter 2, the curtain walls could have been built to a height of 1.2m inside a year. With the castle in such an incomplete state, though theoretically defendable, the platform may have provided a stable position for defenders as opposed to the unfinished sandstone rubble of the rest of the castle.

The Context of Buckton: The Case for Ranulf II

Whilst absolute dating evidence for two construction phases at Buckton Castle is scanty, the stratified pottery and the form of the castle suggest a 12th or early-13th century date for this activity. This is in keeping with the character of Buckton's construction. Chapter 2 showed that building Buckton Castle may have a little over £100, and it seems unlikely

Given the assumption that Buckton was built by an earl of Chester, only a higher authority, namely the king, could have authorised its destruction

Fig 54: The Scottish occupation (in green) of northern England during the reign of King Stephen (1136-54). The lands and castles of the Earl of Chester are also shown.

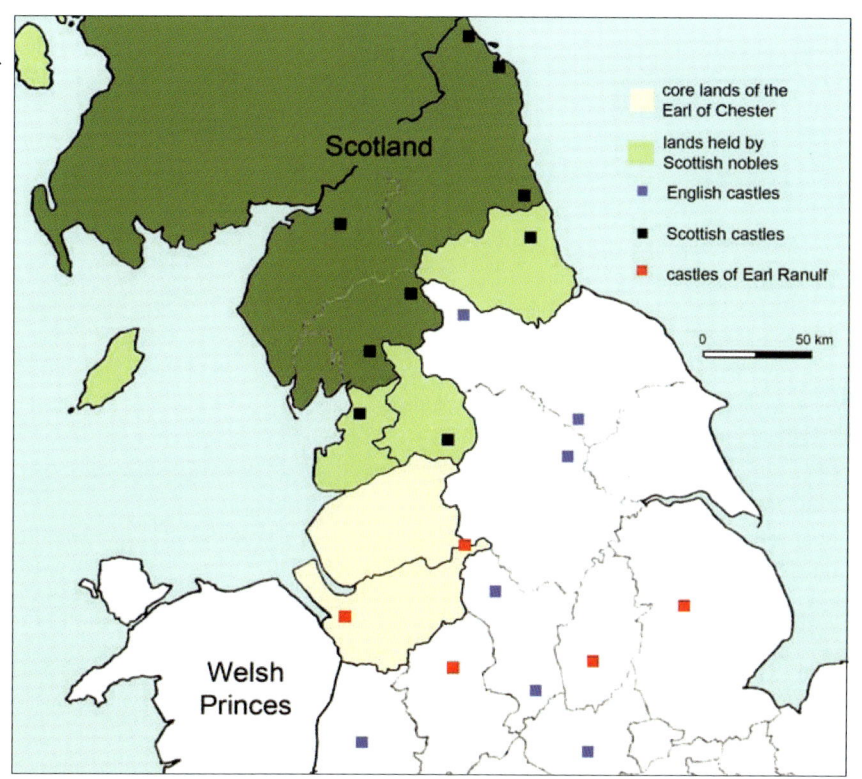

that this work would have been undertaken by anyone other than the earl of Chester. Compared to the other English counties along the Welsh border – Hereford and Shropshire – Cheshire had a small number of castles (Fig 25) which may partly reflect the earls' exercising control over fortification building. Another possibility is that William de Neville may have built Buckton Castle in the 1180s.[27] Between 1181 and 1186 the earl of Chester, Ranulf (III) de Blundeville, granted William de Neville the lordship of Longdendale. The expenditure may not have been beyond his means but it seems unlikely the earl of Chester would have allowed a vassal to build a stone castle on the edge of his territory.

Given the assumption that Buckton was built by an earl of Chester, only a higher authority, namely the king, could have authorised its destruction. Furthermore, the possibly short-lived use of the castle suggests it was built in a period of unrest and slighted soon after. Between

1066 and 1485 there were around 84 instances of castle slightings recorded in England. More than half of these (45) occurred during the reigns of Stephen and Henry II.[28] The destruction of castles was a response to civil unrest, so the civil war of Stephen's reign and the revolt of 1173 to 1174 under Henry II are the most likely periods for Buckton's construction and subsequent destruction. This means that either Earl Ranulf de Gernon or Earl Hugh de Kevelioc was the man responsible for its construction.

During the barons' revolt of 1173-4[29] Earl Hugh took up arms against Henry II. The earl was captured and later restored to his property. While punishing Hugh by slighting Chester Castle was not a realistic option because of its importance as a border fortress, the king could have given it into the custody of someone more reliable. As Henry II chose to trust the earl it seems the two were reconciled while Hugh was held in captivity. But the act of demolition could have a symbolic function and so may have been punitive – the earl did rebel after all – and half of the recorded slightings in the aftermath of the revolt were to castles owned by three of the main rebel earls, the earls of Derby, Leicester, and Suffolk.[30]

While demolishing Buckton may have been punishment for rebelling, even though he was later reconciled with the king, it is also worth considering that Henry II may have been wary about his treatment of the rebels, as demonstrated in the peace treaty in which the barons would retain the property they held before the outbreak of hostilities.[31] However, the earl seems to have received more lenient treatment, probably because of his reconciliation with Henry II.

By far the most satisfying context for the construction of Buckton Castle is the anarchy of the reign of King Stephen (Fig 54). Upon the death of Henry I in 1135 his nephew, Stephen of Blois, seized the English throne. This presented Earl Ranulf with a political problem as he had sworn allegiance to Matilda, Henry I's daughter. Nevertheless Ranulf later swore his loyalty to the new King Stephen. In 1136, the year after the death of Henry I, King David of Scotland, uncle of Matilda, crossed the Scottish border and seized several fortified places in Northumbria but also importantly the stronghold of Carlisle and the district of Cumberland, his army reaching as far south as Clitheroe in the Ribble Valley.[32]

Ranulf, who aspired to the earldom of Carlisle, had to stand by and

By far the most satisfying context for the construction of Buckton Castle is the anarchy of the reign of King Stephen

> **The further loss of lands to the Scots now prompted Earl Ranulf to revolt; the first of seven times**

watch whilst Stephen recognised the Scottish takeover of Carlisle and Cumberland as well as Northumbria in the Treaty of Durham in 1138. Even though Stephen allowed this loss of land, Ranulf initially remained his supporter, probably due to the relationship of Matilda and David. A second Treaty of Durham in 1139 granted David's son the Earldom of Northumbria, the honour of Lancaster and Lancashire north of the Ribble. The further loss of lands to the Scots now prompted Earl Ranulf to revolt; the first of seven times during the 'Anarchy' that he was accused of doing so.[33] Probably the best known revolt was to culminate in the Battle of Lincoln in 1141 when Stephen was captured. Building a castle to protect Cheshire from David thus seems a plausible reason.[34]

Castles in the Air

Whatever the precise date of Buckton Castle's construction, as one of the earliest stone castles in the region, it was built for a specific need. When that need, be it as a symbol of the power and status of the earls of Chester or as a strategic site for their use, was removed so was the need for the castle. One last hint of the context for the raising of Buckton can be found in a folk legend from Longdendale. A local historian, William Chadwick, published in 1870 a story set during the Anarchy.[35] He related how the Empress Matilda, riding northwards in 1139 to meet her uncle, King David of Scotland, stayed a night in the Longdendale Valley, the next valley southwards from Buckton. A great battle was fought where the parish church of St Michael's, Mottram-in-Longdendale, was later built. Matilda lost and was forced to flee, and the site was afterwards known as Warhill. Although this tale is not recorded any earlier than 1870, and there is no archaeological evidence for any battle of this period at Mottram, it is a curious coincidence that Buckton Castle probably dates from the same period. Perhaps a folk memory of these disturbed and violent times lingered as late as the 19th century in this part of Tameside, or was William Chadwick inspired by his knowledge of nearby Buckton?

CHAPTER 4

Buckton after the Castle

Fig 55: An aerial view of Buckton Castle in the mid-1990s showing the pits dug by treasure hunters.

Chapter 4

Buckton after the Castle

Introduction

The earliest documented reference to Buckton Castle captures its transition from a military site to a romantic ruin (Fig 55). In 1360 a survey of the rents and services due from the tenants of the lord of Longdendale mentioned the castle twice. The drafts of this survey survive today in the Public Record Office in London.[1] Written on seven sheets of vellum the notes and crossings outs of the scribe can be seen. On the third membrane, or sheet, was recorded the evidence of the local jurors 'who say upon their oath there is there one ruined castle called Buckeden and of no value'. A draft entry uses the same wording on the seventh membrane.[2] Though in ruins by 1360 Buckton was still recognised as a high status site, being the first entry in the rental. The castle next occurs in the documentary record during the 16th century. Buckton Castle is said to have been the site of a beacon during the Pilgrimage of Grace in 1536-7; a rebellion of the northern counties against Henry VIII's religious reforms. It may also have been used as a beacon site during the invasion scares of the 1580s, particularly in the Armada year of 1588.[3] At the end of the century it was drawn on an estate map of Stayley manor (Fig 56). This map shows a low circuit of stone walling, standing on a hill, described as 'Buckden Castle', the earliest known depiction of the site.[4] The memory of the castle and its importance faded over the following two centuries.

Antiquarian Rediscovery

In the 18th century rumours of buried treasure at the castle began to circulate. In 1730 'country people' spent several days 'in fruitless searching with pick and shovels for the missing treasure'.[5] A more successful hunt in 1767 is recorded in a letter from Mr R Wardleworth, the schoolmaster of Mottram, to John Collier of Milnrow.[6] Wardleworth

> **The earliest documented reference to Buckton Castle captures its transition from a military site to a romantic ruin**

CHAPTER 4

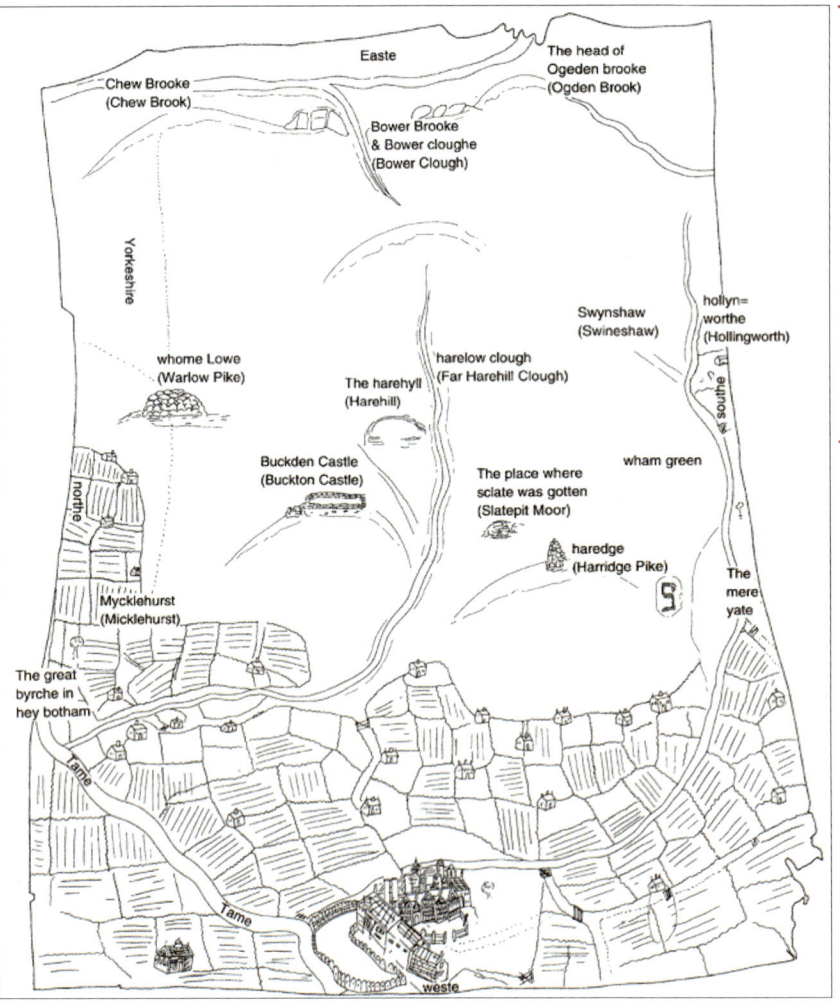

Buckton after the Castle

> **Wardleworth records that some of the local tenants had discovered a golden necklace, a silver vessel, and a lid to the west of the castle**

Fig 56: A transcription of the late 16th century Stayley estate map showing the location of Buckton Castle.

records that some of the local tenants had discovered a golden necklace, a silver vessel, and a lid to the west of the castle during work to widen the roadway which skirts the foot of the Buckton Hill. These details were contained in a letter written on the 11th February 1767 and provide a contemporary account of this discovery:

'I had the favour of yours requesting an answer to certain Queries and Interrogatories concerning some curious Antique Things lately found at Buckton Castle. I sent for the man, whose name is John Hayward, who digged them up, and examined him about the same. There is a cartway under the said Hill, leading from Mottram to Saddleworth, which being thought too narrow, the Inhabitants met to repair and enlarge the same. The said John Hayward, being about the centre of the said Hill, in cutting up a shovel's Graft from the surface, discovered some black wood ashes as he thought them to be. He told his companions that he was got upon some Hearth Stone, and putting his Shovel under the ashes, the Golden Necklace came up, bright and fresh as out of the hands of the maker, 18 Beads as large as Bullocs upon a curious Gold chain, with a Loquet, about the compass of a Moidere, quartered crosswise by 4 sceptres; the whole weighed near 2 ounces Troy.

Another man, about 2 yds distance North, in a right line from the other, at the same time discovered in many Pieces a broken Vessel tarnished of a dusky colour, which he took to be silver, and thought if whole would contain a Quart. It was embossed, and the shape of a Crown upon one part thereof. Whether it was all in pieces before he struck it with his mattock or no he could not tell, but thought it was. A piece of the vessel I procured, & have herein enclosed the same, and send it you.

Also at the same time the same person with the broken vessel throwed up something like a Silver Duster's top, fresh from the Finer. These were the Particular materials then & there found, with the circumstances thereof.

The men Quarrelling about the Property &c and as John Hayward holds a small Farm under Lord Dysart, Ld of the manor, they were informed he would claim them; accordingly they were brought & delivered to the Steward, then in Mottram but who lived in Nantwich, Wickstead, an Attorney, in whose hands I saw them. He gave the man with the necklace a Guinea, & I was informed Mr Lever would have given 10 Guineas for them; the man with the broken vessel, 2s. As the Necklace &c were, like Dear Timmy your inquisitive letter, without date, nor did any Antiquarian or person skilled in such Things see them whilst in our Neighbourhood, I humbly refer the rest to your further observation and more penetrative judgment in things of this Nature...'[7]

A sketch drawn on the letter (Fig 57) shows the approximate location where these finds were made. The subsequent whereabouts of the finds are unknown, though it can be assumed the estate steward, Mr Wickstead, passed them on to Lord Dysart.[8] In 1903 W J Andrew reported

> **the Golden Necklace came up, bright and fresh as out of the hands of the maker**

CHAPTER 4 Buckton after the Castle

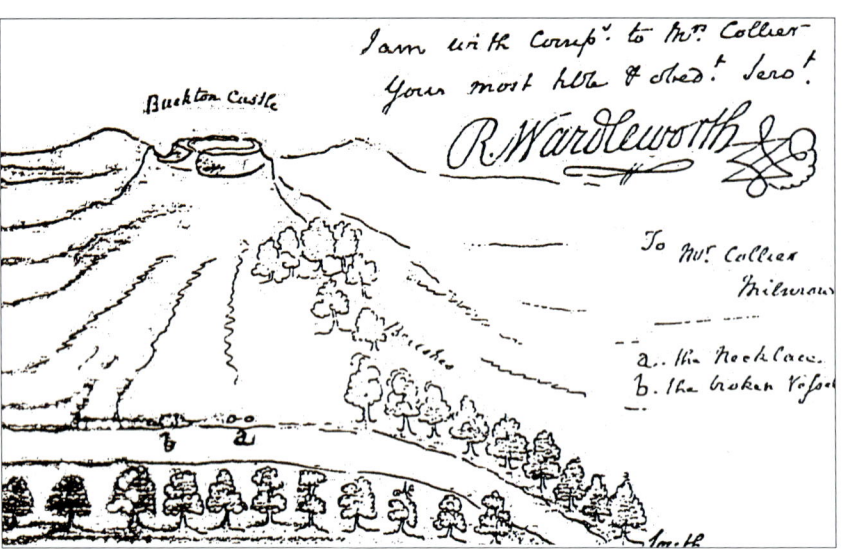

Fig 57: A transcription of Wardleworth's map of the location of the Buckton treasure from 1767. Source; Raines manuscripts, Chetham Library.

that his grandfather saw 'gold beads' discovered during the 1810s close to the castle, which at the very least suggests treasure hunters were still exploring the site at that date.[9]

Wardleworth's sketch from 1767 provided the second view of the castle. This showed the monument from the north-west with an inner bank, topped by what might be ruined walls, a deep ditch, and a single entrance on the northern side of the site. The discovery of these gold objects, which were probably medieval in date, was the spur for several visits by local antiquarians in the later 18th and 19th centuries.

The first antiquarian to visit the site was Thomas Percival who climbed the hill in the early 1770s.[10] Percival described and surveyed the site (Fig 58), and although his records remained largely unpublished his work became the key study for the next century upon which later studies were based. According to Percival the castle was oval in plan with a single entrance on the north-western side. Within the rampart on the eastern side of the enclosure, were the ruins of walls standing up to *c.* 2m high, whilst on the southern side of the enclosure Percival recorded what he believed to have been a well close the rampart. Percival drew attention to the absence of the ditch on the south-western side of the castle. The common assumption has since been that on this side the steep natural slope made a continuation of the ditch unnecessary. However, it was not until a detailed contour survey was undertaken by the

The first antiquarian to visit the site was Thomas Percival who climbed the hill in the early 1770s

University of Manchester in 1996 that this was fully demonstrated. The resultant survey also recorded some slippage along the western slope beneath the curtain wall.[11]

The Reverend John Watson, the rector of Stockport, visited Buckton Castle during the mid-1770s, providing the first published written ac-

Fig 58: The recording of Buckton Castle from the 1770s to the 1940s. These plans were drawn by Thomas Percival (1777), George Ormerod (1817), Saddleworth Geological Society (1842), Canon Francis Robert Raines (mid-19th century), William Farrer and John Turnbull (1908), and Mr Byram (1941).

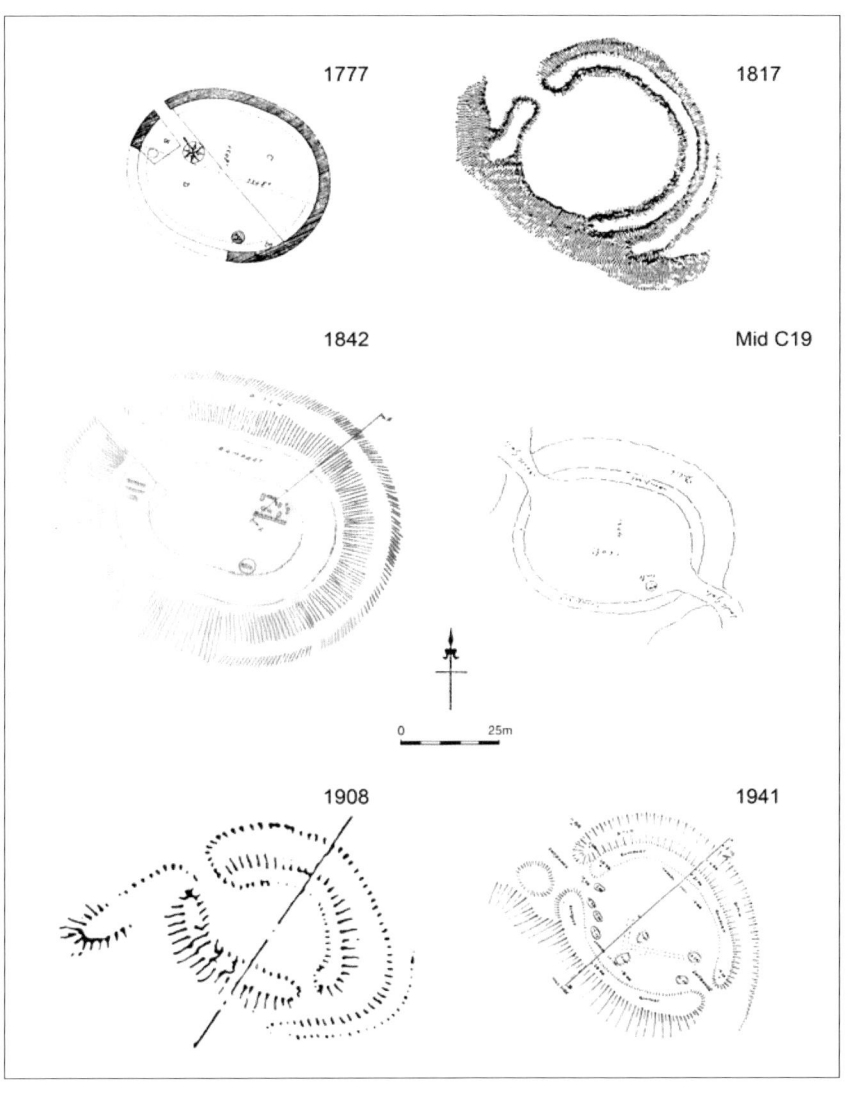

count of the monument in 1777, although using Percival's plan. He recorded that 'the walls are removed, and only a rude heap of stones remains without the least mark of a tool on them, as far as I could observe'.[12] Watson also noted 'the strongest works' appeared to have been on the north-west, just inside the entrance. Watson, however, interpreted the well feature seen by Percival a few years earlier as a robber pit dug by the local tenants. Both Percival and Watson identified further disturbance as a consequence of treasure hunting immediately behind the north-western entrance. From these two accounts it seems clear that by the 1770s much of the interior of castle was already heavily pockmarked from persistent treasure hunting episodes.

In the late-18th and early-19th centuries Buckton Castle was mentioned by several local historians, from John Aikin to James Butterworth but the only new material to be published was a plan and description by George Ormerod (Fig 58) in his three-volume history of Cheshire.[13] Ormerod records that since Percival's drawing was incomplete 'another is substituted, sketched on the spot by the author in 1817'. This new record and his fresh description are important accounts for they are the only substantial record of the landscape to the east of the castle before it was removed by the quarry. He states 'the entrance is on the north-west and a rampart and ditch sweep round from thence on the side nearly level with the rest of the top of the hill to the south-east, where the precipice recommences, and on account of the inequality of the ground, another rampart is here placed outside the ditch in the latter part of its course.'[14] The only other source to mention this second rampart is the Victoria County History for Lancashire in 1908 (Fig 58), by which date 'only worn traces' of the rampart could be seen, probably due to the nearby quarrying activity to the east, which was removing the higher ground beyond the castle.[15]

The growth of local history and natural history studies during the Victorian period had a significant impact on Buckton. This was in part a reaction to the rapid industrialisation of large parts of Britain and in part a result of the increased access to the landscape that the new 11,000 miles of railway track gave to most parts of Britain. By 1885 Buckton lay within walking distance of two railway stations at Mossley, whilst an electric tram service ran close to the site by 1904.[16] Furthermore, a textile village, Carrbrook, was developing at the foot of the hill around the Buckton Vale Print Works (Fig 59).[17] Buckton was no

> **'the walls are removed, and only a rude heap of stones remains without the least mark of a tool on them, as far as I could observe'**

longer an isolated site visited only by the local tenants in search of treasure or antiquarians curious about the origins of the ruins.

The immediate consequence was a growing interest in the castle site. The Saddleworth Geological Society visited the site in the early 1840s and produced a third plan of the site in 1842.[18] This included the location of a ruinous building within the south-eastern part of the enclosure. It is possible that this was the remains of a beacon hut recorded as being built near Mossley around 1803 during the Napoleonic invasion scare of this period. The Geological Society's plan also noted the position of the well noted by Percival in the 1770s and the site of the treasure hunting in 1730. It is perhaps most notable for what it did not show; there was no southern entrance and there was no record of the outer rampart on the eastern side recorded by Ormerod in 1817.

Fig 59: Buckton Castle from the south with the site of the Buckton Vale Print Works at the foot of the hill - now a housing estate.

The most significant of the mid-19th century antiquarians to visit the site was the noted local historian Canon Francis Robert Raines (1805-78), vicar of Milnrow near Rochdale. The south-eastern entrance is first shown on a plan and illustration sketched by the Canon, but more importantly he rediscovered the letter written in 1767 by Wardleworth and preserved it for future generations.[19]

At the end of the century Samuel Andrew published the first detailed, if somewhat rambling, assessment of the castle and also led a tour of the castle for the Lancashire and Cheshire Antiquary Society.[20] In 1892 he reported he had 'found below the castle, on the Saddleworth side, a portion of the road leading to the castle...The pavement in some places still remains undisturbed...On the same side as the pavement lower down the hill there are two deep trenches, not noticed in any account of the place I have seen, probably outworks of the station.'[21] These 'deep trenches' may be the same as 'the trenches at the foot of the hill' which in a report three years later which Andrew later supposed to be evidence of terracing of the hillside for agricultural purposes,[22] although they were removed during the 20th century when a new access road to the quarry was built. The routeway Andrew discovered can still be traced along the slope to the north-west of the castle, and may indeed by an early route up to Buckton.

20th Century Use of the Site

The pattern of treasure-hunting and historical interest in the castle, set during the early-18th century, continued throughout the 20th century. New studies in the middle decades of the century produced a yet another plan,[23] though this one included the most detailed record yet of the robber pits, and articles arguing that the castle was in fact an Iron Age hillfort.[24] Studies of medieval government documents in the 1970s revealed the earliest reference to the castle from 1360. Treasure hunting continued into the early 1980s.[25]

The 20th century also saw two very significant changes to the castle site. Firstly, the massive expansion of the quarry to the east removed the higher ground in this area and the evidence for the second ditch. This quarrying also appears to have disturbed the landscape immediately north of the castle. It created two bank-like features, which were briefly interpreted as an outer bailey [26] until excavations in 1996 re-

The pattern of treasure-hunting and historical interest in the castle, set during the early-18th century, continued throughout the 20th century

Fig 60: A contour survey of Buckton Castle (looking north-west) undertaken in 1996 by the University of Manchester Archaeological Unit. The quarry face can be seen at the bottom of the drawing.

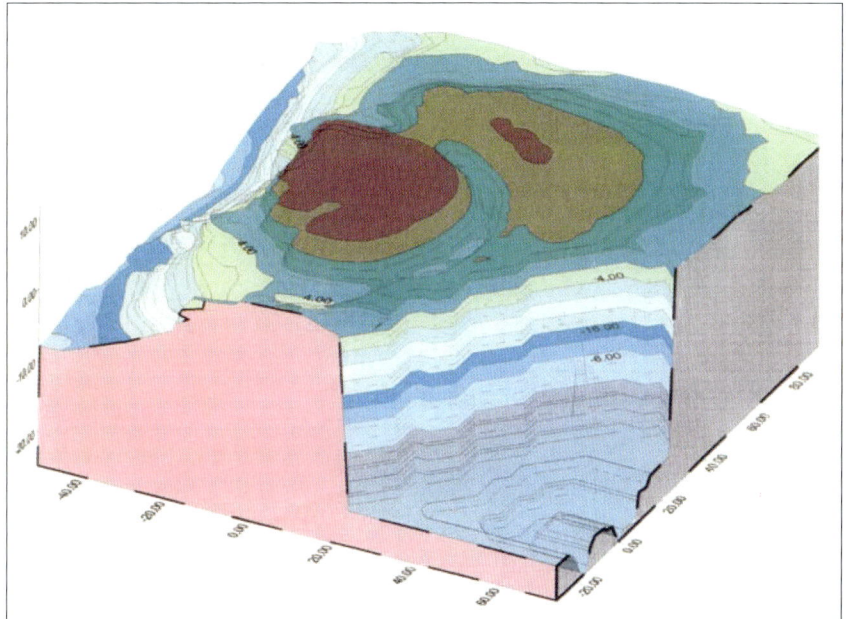

vealed them to be spoil mounds (Fig 60).[27] The growth of the quarry probably led to the site being protected as a scheduled ancient monument in 1924, and is the main reason the site survived into the early-21st century. Secondly, the castle area was used during the Second World War as part of the anti-bomber defences for the Manchester city region, and remains of this protection system can still be seen around the monument.

A World War Two passive anti-aircraft decoy defence system, known as 'Special Fire', with the codename 'Starfish', is recorded in Mossley close to the castle.[28] Following the German bomber raid on Coventry during the night of the 14th November 1940, a large number of Starfiish decoys were constructed.[29] Positioned along suspected bomber routes some four miles in advance of probable targets, these sites typically consisted of mock buildings containing highly combustible material. There were nine permanent Starfish sites in the Manchester region, one of which was located in Mossley area; in other words at Buckton. The earliest reference to this decoy site at Mossley was 1st August 1941 and the last reference was 8th April 1943.[30]

As a raid commenced the flammable material would be ignited electrically from a central shelter, sited some distance from these structures (often about 365m), in order to mimic bomb damage and encourage false attacks. The central shelter or command post typically consisted of a small brick-built structure on a concrete foundation, sometimes with a separate generator building attached, and is the only substantial structure to survive on such sites. However, it is possible evidence relating to the firebreak trenches, which surrounded some of the fire displays, may survive as earthworks or crop marks; but these have not been looked for in the vicinity of Buckton Castle because of the encroachment of the quarry onto the Starfish site. In 1942 Starfish sites were given rocket protectors and mobile sites were introduced. By the end of 1943, with a decrease in enemy activity, the decoy sites went out of use.

The site contains three structures that relate to this phase of activity; a small concrete foundation for a brick-built structure, *c.* 4m by 6m on the southern edge of the castle ditch; a short stretch of bank next to the concrete base and running eastwards from the earthwork; and a length of cast guttering recovered from one of the 1996 trenches dug to the north of the castle. The first of these features appears to be shown on an RAF aerial photograph of the site taken in the late 1940s. This also shows a circuit of trackway, immediately north of the quarry, leading up to this concrete platform.

Re-inventing Buckton for the 21st Century

The archaeological excavations from 2007 to 2010 finally demonstrated that Buckton was a stone castle, that it had not been occupied for very long and, perhaps, that it had never been completed. Its primary purpose did not last long, as indicated by the collapse, deliberate or otherwise, of the curtain wall into the ditch. Thereafter the castle lay in ruins, gradually being reclaimed by the heather moorland from which it had been dug. It remained a prominent landscape feature on the edge of Buckton Moor, dominating the middle Tame Valley. As the memory of its original use faded, rumours of gold and silver hidden around the monument grew. The site even had a defensive role to play during the 20th century, which perhaps echoed part of its original function. The twin interests of the treasure hunter and the antiquarian remain into the 21st century. During the life of the current research project, from 1995 to 2012, there have been two recorded instances of treasure hunting

The archaeological excavations from 2007 to 2010 finally demonstrated that Buckton was a stone castle

Fig 61: Local community volunteers celebrate the end of the 2010 excavation season in the castle ditch.

damage on the monument. Yet during the same period dozens of local volunteers (Fig 61) have been involved in the rediscovery through excavation and survey of Buckton Castle, some of them going on to found their own local society[31] (the Tameside Archaeological Society). This 17 years of work has ensured a more scientific understanding of Buckton will be carried into the 21st century, helping to secure the castle for future generations through a better understanding of its local and regional importance.

Fig 62: Clitheroe Castle. Image courtesy of Lancashire County Council.

Chapter 5

A Gazetteer of the Castle Sites of North West England

Introduction

The following gazetteer lists the main information relating to each castle in North West England, including location and setting, owners, foundation, fate, and significant events. Where these are not included, they are probably unknown or uncertain. They are divided by their status at their foundation, although this does not necessarily reflect later ownership. For example Brough began as a royal castle but was later granted to members of the nobility. Castle Sowerby (NY360384) and Shocklach No. 2 (SJ434509) are included in *Castellarium Anglicanum*, but have been rejected as castle sites.[1] Late 20th century county divisions have been used to describe their location. Gazetteer numbers refer to the castle distribution map at the end of this volume E = excavated.

Royal

(1) Brough, Cumbria (NY 791 141), was built within the ruins of a Roman fort on the route between Carlisle and York. Probably first built after 1092 when William II conquered northern Westmorland and Cumberland, some 11th century masonry survives. Brough Castle was captured and damaged in 1174 by the Scottish King William the Lion. Documentary evidence suggests the castle was repaired between 1199 and 1202, and it is from this period that most of the extant ruins date. In 1204, King John gave Brough to Roger de Vieuxpont; although the castle was in a state of disrepair by 1245. The castle was remodelled in the late-13th and 14th century. Both Edward I and Edward II visited and during the Anglo-Scottish Wars the castle was a place of refuge for the locality. The castle came into the Clifford family by marriage in the 14th century and remained with them barring a short time during the Wars

> Brough began as a royal castle but was later granted to members of the nobility

of the Roses. The castle burned down in 1521 during a Christmas feast and remained in a ruinous state until the mid-17th century when it was partially restored by Lady Anne Clifford, but thereafter declined.[2] Substantial masonry remains include the keep and outer gatehouse *E*.

(2) Carlisle, Cumbria (NY 397 563), was built over part of a Roman fort at the confluence of three rivers and the junction of roads between England and Scotland. It was founded by William II in 1092, though there may have been a small castle pre-dating that built by William. Henry I instigated the construction of the keep, which still stands today, and rebuilt the wooden castle in stone. In 1135 it was captured by King David I of Scotland. Henry II reclaimed Carlisle from the Scots in 1157. William the Lion unsuccessfully attacked the castle in 1173 and 1174. Henry II visited in 1186, and King John stayed four times during his reign. Working with the discontented English barons against John, Alexander II of Scotland captured the castle in 1216; the Scottish forces withdrew after John's death. During the Anglo-Scottish Wars, Edward I visited the castle several times due to its proximity to the border. After the Battle of Bannockburn in 1315, the Scots unsuccessfully besieged Carlisle. By 1335, the castle was in a dilapidated state, but in the early-15th century it experienced renewed importance as the centre of the Western March and large sums were spent on ensuring the castle was well-defended. However Carlisle received little investment in the early Tudor period and a survey of 1529 reflects the castle's neglected state. Carlisle Castle was attacked during the Pilgrimage of Grace, and Henry VIII modernised the town and castle defences, introducing new styles of fortification and gun batteries.[3] It was besieged during the Civil War and again during the Jacobite rebellion. The castle is still in use today and there are substantial masonry remains that include the keep and the inner and outer gatehouses *E*.

(3) Chester, Cheshire (SJ 404 657), built just outside the walls of the Roman town and overlooking a bend in the River Dee, was founded by William the Conqueror in about 1070, marking the town as an administrative and military centre in the region. In 1071, the town and castle were given over to Hugh, the new Earl of Chester. From then on it descended through the Earldom, which came under permanent royal control in 1237. Due to its proximity to the Anglo-Welsh border it was used as a base for expeditions into Wales, and in the 12th century for missions to Ireland. In 1265, Simon de Montfort captured the castle,

After the Battle of Bannockburn in 1315, the Scots unsuccessfully besieged Carlisle

> After Edward I conquered Wales in the later 13th century, Chester Castle became less important militarily but was maintained by the Crown

and royal forces embarked on a successful ten-week siege to retake it. After Edward I conquered Wales in the later 13th century, Chester Castle became less important militarily but was maintained by the Crown. In 1400 rebels unsuccessfully besieged the castle; afterwards Chester again lost military importance and was primarily used for administration and to hold court. The castle was held by Royalist forces during the Civil War, and after avoiding damage surrendered in 1646.[4] It remains in use today but little survives of the medieval fabric, beyond the motte, although the Agricola Tower dates from the late 12th century *E*.

Aristocratic

(4) Appleby, Cumbria (NY 686 199), was founded as a timber motte and bailey by Ranulf de Meschines before he became earl of Chester in 1120 and between 1120 and 1121 was taken under royal control. The castle was captured by the Scots in 1136 under whose control it remained until 1157 when the Scottish king, Malcolm, returned it to English royal control. Appleby was given to the Moreville family before William of Scotland captured the castle in 1174. It was granted to the Vieuxpont family, who also owned the castles of Brough and Brougham, in 1203. A Scottish army attack Appleby in 1314 and 1388; in 1539 the castle was described as ruinous although was still used as a prison.[5] Still a residence. Masonry remains, including the keep.

(5) Beeston, Cheshire (SJ 537 593) (Fig 63), was founded by the earl of Chester in the 1220s. Built overlooking the rural Cheshire plain, it

Fig 63: Nathaniel and Samuel Buck's view of Beeston Castle form 1727.

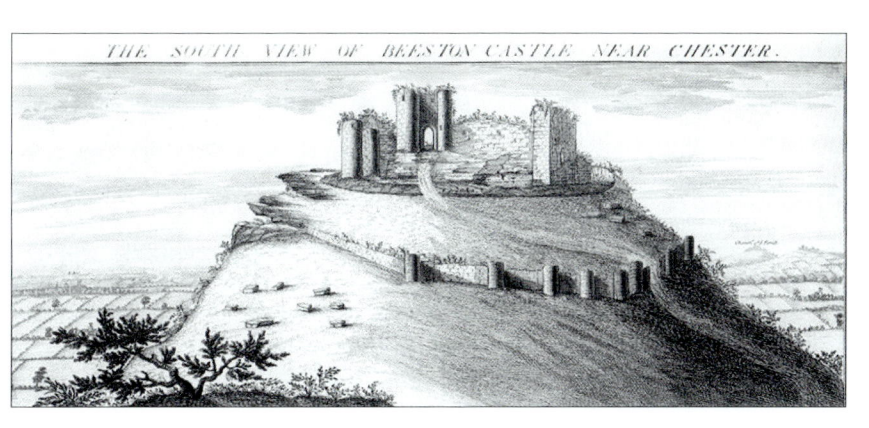

was taken into the possession of the Crown in 1237. The Crown sold the castle in the early-17th century, and it was slighted during the Civil War.[6] The substantial masonry remains include the outer gatehouse with D-shaped towers, outer bailey curtain wall and the inner gatehouse, which has two large D-shaped towers *E*.

(6) Brougham, Cumbria (NY 537 290), sits at the confluence of the river Eamont and Lowther and the junction of three Roman roads. It was built at one end of a Roman fort by Robert Vieuxpont, owner of Brough Castle, in the early-13th century. Vieuxpont's descendant rebelled against the Crown during the Second Baron's War and Henry III confiscated Brougham Castle. The family lands were later returned and the castle passed into the ownership of the Clifford family with whom Brougham Castle would remain. Edward I probably visited in 1300. The castle was captured by the Scots in 1388.[7] The ruined masonry remains include the complex gatehouse and the keep *E*.

(7) Buckton, Greater Manchester (SD 989 016), see Chapter 3.

(8) Greenhalgh, Lancashire (SD 501 451), was built by the earl of Derby, who received a licence to crenellate in 1490. Greenhalgh has an unusual plan, with "elements of both tower keep and quadrangular castle". It was besieged and damaged during the English Civil War.[8] Fragmentary masonry remains of the keep survive *E*.

Fig 64: Aerial view of Lancaster Castle looking east. Image courtesy of Lancashire County Council.

Fig 65: Aerial view of Shotwick Castle. © Cheshire Archaeology Planning Advisory Service.

(9) Lancaster, Lancashire (SD 611 789) (Fig 64), lies over the remains of a Roman fort on a hill overlooking the town and a crossing point of the River Lune. It was founded as a timber castle in 1093 by Roger of Poitou, a kinsman of William II and a powerful landowner. Henry I confiscated the castle and Roger's lands in 1102 after he supported a pretender to the crown. It changed ownership several times, passing in and out of royal control. The great stone keep was likely built in the mid-12th century, and the rest of the castle was rebuilt in stone in the early-12th century under the Crown. Lancaster Castle was damaged in the Scottish raids in Lancashire of 1322 and 1389. The monumental gatehouse was added at the start of the 15th century. The castle remained peacefully in the hands of the Crown until the Civil War when it was taken by Parliamentarian forces.[9] Although partially rebuilt in the early 19th century the keep, monumental gatehouse, and some of the curtain wall survives.

> **Lancaster Castle was damaged in the Scottish raids in Lancashire of 1322 and 1389**

(10) Liverpool, Merseyside (SJ 343 903), was probably built by William de Ferrers, third earl of Derby (d. 1190). The castle was confiscated by the Crown in the late-13th century when Robert de Ferrers, sixth earl of Derby rebelled against Henry III. In 1315 the castle and borough of Liverpool were given to Baron Robert de Holand. Adam Banaster, a retainer of the earl of Lancaster, unsuccessfully assaulted the castle the same year. After the earl was executed in 1322, the castle returned to the control of the Crown. Edward II stayed at the castle for a week in 1323. Later on Liverpool Castle was mostly used as a prison.[10] Site has been built over and there are no above ground remains *E*.

(11) Penrith, Cumbria (NY 512 299), is traditionally ascribed to William Strickland based on licences to crenellate from 1397 to 1399, shortly before he became Bishop of Carlisle. However, in 2008 Perriam postulated that the licences post-date the construction of the castle, and that it was more likely built in the 1380s by Ralph Neville, of the powerful northern dynasty. By 1471 it was in the possession of Richard, Duke of Gloucester, later King Richard III, who undertook building work at the castle. A survey of 1565 recorded Penrith as being in a ruinous state.[11] The substantial masonry remains include the square courtyard buildings *E*.

(12) Shotwick, Cheshire (SJ 350 704) (Fig 65), was built near a fording point on the River Dee. It was first mentioned in 1240, though common tradition holds that it was founded by one of the Earls of Chester, possibly in the late-11th century. In royal control from 1237. Edward I and the Black Prince stayed in 1278 and 1353 respectively.[12] Earthwork remains only, although excavations in the 1990s demonstrated that there was a stone inner bailey *E*.

Baronial

(13) Aldford, Cheshire (SJ 419 596), sits along a Roman road and overlooks a crossing point of the River Dee close to the Anglo-Welsh border. Its foundation date is uncertain, although a Norman piscina discovered in 1959 may suggest the castle is Norman.[13] It is unclear when the castle was abandoned. Only the earthen motte remains *E*.

(14) Aldingham, Cumbria (SD 278 698), stands on a bluff on the coast of Morecambe Bay, overlooking a route across the sands. Excavations carried out in 1968 discovered early-12th-century pot sherds associated with the earliest phase, suggesting it was built by Michael le Fleming, the lord of Aldingham Forest. There were two subsequent building phases in the mid-12th and early-13th centuries.[14] A lack of further archaeological evidence suggests the castle was abandoned, perhaps a generation after the last building phase. Earthwork remains *E*.

(15) Arkholme-with-Cawood, Lancashire (SD 589 718), is a motte, probably with a bailey, sitting close to a river. The motte has two dis-

> Aldford...sits along a Roman road and overlooks a crossing point of the River Dee close to the Anglo-Welsh border

Fig 66: The conserved southern wall of Bury Castle. Image courtesy of Greater Manchester Archaeological Advisory Service.

tinct layers, indicating more than one building phase and extended use. Probably dating from the Norman period, Arkholme and nearby Melling Castle controlled a strategic river crossing.[15] Earthwork remains *E*.

(16) Askerton, Cumbria (NY 550 693), was founded in the 15th century, and was rebuilt in 1485–1525 by Thomas, Lord Dacre. The castle was in decay by 1580.[16] Masonry remains.

(17) Beaumont, Cumbria (NY 348 593), is a motte and bailey castle on the banks of the River Eden, and on the remains of the Roman wall. Its history is obscure, although Robert the Bruce may have used the site in 1322 when he invaded England.[17] Earthwork remains.

(18) Blackrod, Greater Manchester (SD 619 106), was excavated by the University of Manchester in the 1950s, however no dating material was recovered, and little is known about this site.[18] Earthwork remains *E*.

(19) Bewcastle, Cumbria (NY 566 747), was built within a Roman fort. First mentioned in 1378 it was captured by the Scots then retaken by the English in 1401. Abandoned by 1478.[19] Masonry remains.

(20) Brampton, Cumbria (NY 533 612), is a motte with an obscure history, though it was used as a beacon in 1468.[20] Earthwork remains.

(21) Bury, Greater Manchester (SD 803 108) (Fig 66), was a manor house fortified by Sir Thomas Pilkington who was granted a licence to

CHAPTER 5 Excavation and Survey at Buckton Castle

105

crenellate in 1469. After the Pilkington family supported the House of York in the Wars of the Roses, Henry Tudor ordered the demolition of Bury Castle.[21] Excavations have revealed masonry remains of the outer curtain wall *E*.

(22) Castle Banks, Lancashire (SD 824 498), was not included in *Castellarium Anglicanum*, but was identified as a castle by Higham through the use of place-name evidence. She suggested this site at Gisburne in the upper Ribble Valley and the nearby Castle Haugh would have controlled the Ribble Valley and the major route through the area.[22] Earthwork remains.

(23) Castle Haugh, Lancashire (SD 830 507), is a small castle in the upper Ribble Valley with an obscure history. Higham suggests that Castle Haugh and Castle Banks would have controlled the Ribble Valley and the major route through the area.[23] Earthwork remains.

(24) Castle Hill, Lancashire (SD 522 536), sits near a river crossing in Dolphinholme. Not included in *Castellarium* Anglicanum, it was identified as a castle by Higham through the use of place-name evidence. Although a motte survives, the site's history is obscure.[24]

(25) Clitheroe, Lancashire (SD 743 417) (Fig 62), is located on a rocky outcrop overlooking the town. The foundation date is uncertain, as is the person responsible. While some such as those responsible for the National Monuments Record and the Lancashire Towns Survey consider it likely to have been in existence by 1102, Cathcart King believes the charter refers to another location. It was owned by the Lacy family until 1311, when it came into the possession of the House of Lancaster. Clitheroe had a generally peaceful history, although when Adam Banaster, a retainer of the earl of Lancaster, revolted against his lord in 1315 he captured the castle. It was slighted during the English Civil War.[25] The masonry remains include the keep and inner bailey *E*.

(26) Cockermouth, Cumbria (NY 122 309), lay close to the coast. Its foundation date is unclear. It was not documented until 1221, but may well have been built as early as the 1130s. The castle was rebuilt in stone in the mid-13th century. It was maintained by its owners and besieged in 1648 although it did not fall.[26] Masonry remains.

(27) Dodleston, Cheshire (SJ 361 608), is a motte and bailey with little recorded history.[27] Earthwork remains.

(28) Down Hall, Cumbria (NY 283 525), is a medieval manor house

> Clitheroe...was owned by the Lacy family until 1311, when it came into the possession of the House of Lancaster

of which no masonry survives above ground *E*.[28]

(29) Dunham Massey, Greater Manchester (SJ 734 874) (Fig 67), was one of three castles in north-east Cheshire controlled by the de Massey family. It was the administrative centre of the family's estates. The castle was first documented in 1173 when Hamon de Massey held Dunham Massey and Ullerwood castles against Henry II. Dunham Massey Castle may have been standing as late as 1323.[29] The motte was probably re-used as a prospect mound in the 16th century.

(30) Egremont, Cumbria (NY 011 102), probably dates from the 12th century. In the words of Cathcart King, it has "little history", and was first mentioned in 1203. Originally a timber castle, it was rebuilt in stone in the 13th or 14th century. In 1570 it was recorded as abandoned.[30] Masonry remains.

(31) Frodsham, Cheshire (SJ 514 775), is first referred to in the mid-13th century. The new town was probably created in the early 13th century by Ranulf de Blundevile, Earl of Chester and he may have been responsible for building the castle. In 1355 it was recorded as being in need of repair and in 1654 it burnt down, leaving no visible remains.[31]

(32) Gleaston, Cumbria (SD 262 715), stands on a hill overlooking the village of the same name. It may have been built as a successor to

Fig 67: The motte, later a prospect mound, outside Dunham Hall, Dunham Massey. Image courtesy of Norman Redhead.

Aldingham Castle, and probably dates from the 14th century. Abandoned in 1458, it was later dismantled.[32] Masonry remains.

(33) Hall Hill, Lancashire (SD 663 468), was not included in *Castellarium Anglicanum*, however it was identified as a possible castle site by Higham through the use of place-name evidence.[33] Earthworks.

(34) Halton, Cheshire (SJ 537 820), is usually attributed to Nigel, baron of Halton, sometime around 1071. It is thought the timber motte and bailey castle was rebuilt in stone in the 12th century. By 1650 it was in a ruined state although it continued in use until the early-20th century.[34] Masonry remains of both the inner and outer bailey *E*.

(35) Halton Castle Hill, Lancashire (SD 500 648), is in a village on a spur of the Cote Beck Valley.[35] Earthwork remains.

(36) Haresceugh, Cumbria (NY 610 428), is an obscure rectangular castle.[36] Fragmentary masonry remains.

(37) Hartley, Cumbria (NY 782 082), sits near the confluence of two streams. Thomas Musgrave received a licence to crenellate his manor house in 1353. It was captured and destroyed by the Scots, and licensed again in 1360.[37] Masonry remains.

(38) Hawes Bridge, Cumbria (SD 513 892), is near a river crossing. Although it was not included in *Castellarium Anglicanum* Higham identified it as a possible castle site through the use of place-name evidence.[38] Earthworks.

(39) Hayes, Cumbria (NY 001 226), was built by Robert de Leyburn who was granted a licence to crenellate his property in 1322, recorded as Aykhurst. It was ruined by 1392.[39] Fragmentary masonry remains.

(40) Hayton, Cumbria (NY 507 578), is of unknown origin, but Jackson suggests it may have been built in the 12th century, after Henry II gave the area to the de Vaux family.[40] Masonry remains.

(41) Highhead, Cumbria (NY 403 433), first mentioned in 1322, this wooden building was replaced by a stone structure when William Lengleys was granted a licence to crenellate in 1342.[41] No visible remains.

(42) Hornby, Lancashire (SD 587 686), in the Lune Valley probably existed by 1229, though there may be an earlier reference from 1205. It is uncertain when it was built, though it was probably founded soon after Montbegon family acquired the lordship. Administratively, the castle was at the centre of the Honour of Hornby.[42] Masonry remains.

(43) Hornby/Castlestede, Lancashire (SD 583 698), (Fig 68) is a

---

Kendal Castle How…is traditionally attributed to the late-11th century, possibly built by Gilbert de Lancaster

Fig 68: Aerial view of Castlestede, Hornby in the Lune Valley. Image courtesy of Lancashire County Council.

motte and bailey that was probably the precursor to the 13th-century castle at Hornby. It overlooks a medieval river crossing beyond the village; the castle most likely dates from the 11th or 12th century.[43] Earthwork remains including the motte *E*.

(44) Irthington, Cumbria (NY 499 615), is an obscure motte and bailey.[44] Earthwork remains.

(45) Kendal Castle How, Cumbria (SD 512 924), is traditionally attributed to the late-11th century, possibly built by Gilbert de Lancaster. Abandoned around 1184.[45] Earthwork remains *E*.

(46) Kendal, Cumbria (SD 522 924), succeeded Kendal Castle How in around 1184 and was built by the de Lancaster family. Originally a timber castle, it was rebuilt in stone in the 13th century. Kendal Castle was surrendered to King John in 1216. It passed through several families, the fitz Reinfred, the Lancasters, the de Brus, de Roos, and the Parrs. In 1566 the castle was abandoned and diosmantled.[46] Fragmentary masonry remains, including the curtain wall and gatehouse *E*.

(47) Kirkby Lonsdale, Cumbria (SD 611 789), is a motte situated next to a river with almost no recorded history.[47] Earthwork remains.

(48) Kirkoswald, Cumbria (NY 559 410), was first mentioned in 1201 when Sir Hugh de Morville was granted a licence to crenellate.

Cathcart King believes the fabric of the building dates from the 14th century, though in 1485 it was recorded as "newly built".[48] Masonry remains.

(49) Liddel Strength, Cumbria (NY 402 742), was first mentioned in 1174 when it was captured by the Scottish king, William the Lion. It was captured by the Scots again in 1319 and 1346, but soon after abanadoned.[49] Earthwork remains, including a large motte.

(50) Macclesfield, Cheshire (SJ 917 736), was a manor house fortified by John de Macclesfield, Keeper of the Great Wardrobe under Richard II. John was given a license to crenellate in 1410. Macclesfield Castle was later owned by the Dukes of Buckingham and the Earls of Derby before falling out of use in the 16th century.[50] No visible remains.

(51) Malpas, Cheshire (SJ 486 472), was probably built by Robert Fitzhugh soon after the Norman Conquest. The town was the seat of the barons of Malpas.[51] A prominent motte lies next to the church.

(52) Manchester, Greater Manchester (SJ 839 989), sat on a bluff overlooking the confluence of the rivers Irk and Irwell, next to the medieval church. The castle was first documented in 1184 and belonged to the Greley family, lords of Manchester.[52] No visible remains *E*.

(53) Maryport, Cumbria (NY 033 362), has an obscure history. Excavations in 1914 produced 14th century pottery, although the Scheduled Monument Record lists the site as 12th century.[53] Earthwork remains.

54) Melling, Lancashire (SD 599 712), is a motte in the centre of a village on the south side of the Lune Valley. Probably dating from the Norman period, Melling and the nearby castle of Arkholme controlled a strategic river crossing.[54] Earthwork remains.

(55) Millom, Cumbria (SD 171 813), first mentioned 1335 when John de Hodleston was granted a licence to crenellate.[55] Masonry remains.

(56) Morhull, Lancashire (SD 516 724), is probably the castle of Merhull that was surrendered by Gilbert Fitz Reinfred to King John in 1216.[56] No visible remains.

(57) Nantwich, Cheshire (SJ 651 523), is usually ascribed to William Malbank, who received the manor from Hugh d'Avranches, earl of Chester in the 11th century. It is uncertain when it fell out of use, but excavations revealed silting in the castle ditch suggesting its decline began in the 13th and 14th centuries.[57] No visible remains *E*.

(58) Naworth, Cumbria (NY 560 626), was first referenced in 1335

> **Liddel Strength…was first mentioned in 1174 when it was captured by the Scottish king, William the Lion**

> Malpas...near the Welsh border was probably built by Robert Fitzhugh soon after the Norman Conquest

when Ranulph de Dacre, the first Baron Dacre, was granted a licence to crenellate. Naworth Castle successfully resisted an attack from Scottish forces in 1346. It descended through the Dacre family and was in use in the 16th century.[58] Masonry remains including the keep and curtain wall.

(59) Newton-le-Willows, Merseyside (SJ 596 962), sits at the confluence of the River Deane and the Mellingford Brook. Although it was mostly likely the administrative centre of a barony, the site's history is unknown.[59] Earthwork remains.

(60) Northwich, Cheshire (SJ 653 735), was mentioned in the 1190s. Little is known about the castle's history and it is now vanished. Shaw and Clark in the Cheshire Towns Survey question whether it existed at all.[60] No visible remains.

(61) Oldcastle, Cheshire (SJ 468 441), sits on a promontory in the Wych Brook Valley. Its history is unknown, but an 11th or 12th century date for its construction has been suggested based on its proximity to the Anglo-Welsh border.[61] Earthwork remains *E*.

(62) Pendragon, Cumbria (NY 782 026), was probably founded in the 12th century, although it was first documented in 1228. Lady Anne

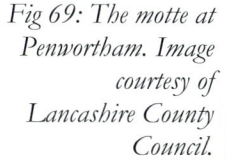

Fig 69: The motte at Penwortham. Image courtesy of Lancashire County Council.

Clifford, who owned the castle in the 17th century, asserted it was captured and destroyed in 1341, and is the earliest surviving source to have made this claim. She believed the castle was abandoned afterwards.[62] Masonry remains of the keep survive.

(63) Pennington, Cumbria (SD 258 777), sits next to the stream of Pennington Beck. Little is known about the site's history.[63] Earthwork remains *E*.

(64) Penwortham, Lancashire (SD 524 291) (Fig 69), is the only castle in North West England recorded in the Domesday Book, although its precise foundation date is unknown. Overlooking a bend in the River Ribble, the castle was the centre of the Barony of Penwortham. It was abandoned by 1232.[64] A large motte survives next to the parish church *E*.

(65) Preston, Lancashire (SD 523 301), was built on a cliff near the River Ribble. When the castle was founded is uncertain, however it is recorded that by 1123 it was granted to Stephen of Blois by King Henry I as part of the Honour of Lancaster; by this point it was abandoned.[65] No visible remains.

(66) Pulford, Cheshire (SJ 375 587), was first mentioned in the late-12th century, and orders were probably given to hold the castle against Owen Glendower in 1403.[66] Earthwork remains include a small motte.

(67) Rochdale, Greater Manchester (SD 892 128), sits on high ground above the River Roch. By the time it was first recorded in 1322 it had long been abandoned.[67] Earthwork remains but partially built over *E*.

(68) Runcorn, Cheshire (SJ 508 833), is listed by Cathcart King as a vanished castle, destroyed in 1862. The location is unknown but according to the Cheshire HER there may have been a Norman castle on the site of a Saxon burh at Runcorn for a while.[68] No visible remains.

(69) Scaleby, Cumbria (NY 449 625), was mentioned in 1307 when Robert de Tylliol was granted a licence to crenellate his "dwelling place". The castle was rebuilt in the 15th century with a wing added in 16th century added. A survey of 1580 recorded it as partly decayed.[69] Masonry remains *E*.

(70) Shipbrook, Cheshire (SJ 674 711), was built near a river. Husain suggested it was one of several castles built along the Anglo-Welsh border during the Welsh Wars.[70] No visible remains.

> **Penwortham....is the only castle in North West England recorded in the Domesday Book**

Fig 70: The motte known as Watch Hill, on the River Bollin. Image courtesy of Norman Redhead.

(71) Shocklach Oldcastle, Cheshire (SJ 433 508), was built near a small stream flowing towards the Anglo-Welsh frontier. It may have been mentioned in 1290 and 1327; however those documents may refer to the later fortified manor house built close by at Shocklach.[71] Earthwork remains include a probable motte.

(72) Stockport, Greater Manchester (SJ 897 905), overlooked the medieval core of the town of the same name, on the banks of the River Mersey at an ancient fording point. The first mention of the castle occurs in 1173, when it is recorded that Geoffrey de Constentin held it against Henry II. There is no further record of Stockport Castle being in use, and historian Arrowsmith suggests it was abandoned by the 14th century.[72] No visible remains *E*.

(73) Tebay, Cumbria (NY 614 051), is a motte and bailey first mentioned in 1200. There is another earthwork nearby, Greenholme at NY600054 which may represent another motte which together with Tebay Castle would have guarded the Birbeck and Lune passes.[73] Earthwork remains include the motte and part of a bailey.

(74) Thurland, Lancashire (SD 610 730), was licensed in 1402, when Sir Thomas Tunstall was given permission to "crenellate his manor". It sits on low ground near the confluence of the rivers Greta and Lune. The castle was besieged and partially destroyed in the English Civil War.[74] Some masonry remains, but the site was extensively rebuilt in the 19th century.

(75) Triermain, Cumbria (NY594 668), was mentioned in 1340 when Roland de Vaux was granted a licence to crenellate his "dwelling place". Its history is obscure, but a survey in 1580 records that the castle was in ruins.[75] Masonry remains.

(76) Ullerwood, Greater Manchester (SJ 799 838), was one of three castles in north-east Cheshire controlled by the de Massey family. It is recorded that Hamon de Massey held the castles of Ullerwood and Dunham Massey against Henry II in 1173.[76] Earthwork remains of the motte, which has been partially built over.

(77) Warrington, Cheshire (SJ 616 885), was a motte and bailey and the home of the lords of Warrington until the castle was burned down in 1260.[77] Some earthwork remains *E*.

(78) Watch Hill, Greater Manchester (SJ 748 860) (Fig 70), was one of three castles controlled by the de Massey family. It overlooks a point where the Roman road between Manchester and Chester crossed the River Mersey. Though Watch Hill is not explicitly recorded, Dunham and Ullerwood are known to have existed by 1173 when Hamon de Massey held them against King Henry II. The only dating evidence from the site is a coin from the reign of Henry II, and it is possible Watch Hill is contemporaneous with the other two de Massey castles. Watch Hill was disused by the 13th century.[78] Excavated in the 1970s. Earthwork remains include the motte and a bailey.

(79) West Derby, Merseyside (SJ 397 935), stands at the confluence of two small streams. It was built before 1232 when it came into possession of the earls of Derby; however it was ruined by 1296. Adam Banaster assaulted West Derby Castle in 1315.[79] Earthwork remains *E*.

(80) Whittington, Lancashire (SD 600 763), is a motte in the Lune Valley.[80] Earthwork remains *E*.

Religious

(81) Piel, Cumbria (SD 233 636) (Fig 71), may have been built in the 12th century as, according to the monks in 1403, King Stephen granted the abbot a licence. Piel Castle was besieged in 1316, 1317, and 1322. In 1327, the abbot of Furness was granted a licence to crenellate his "dwelling-place". The castle was partially dismantled in 1403 due to the cost of maintenance. After the Dissolution of the Monasteries, the

> Watch Hill...was one of three castles in north east Cheshire controlled by the de Massey family

Fig 71: An aerial view of Piel Castle. Image courtesy of Cumbria County Council.

castle was abandoned.[81] Substantial masonry remains iblcude the keep and the curtain wall *E*.

(82) Rose, Cumbria (NY 371 462), was fortified by the Bishop of Carlisle after he receiving a license to crenellate a pre-existing building in 1336. The previous structure was captured and damaged by the Scots in 1314 and 1322.[82] Rose Castle was partly destroyed during the Civil War. Masonry remains.

(83) Wolsty, Cumbria (NY 104 505), was first mentioned in 1348 when the abbot of Holm Cultram Abbey was granted a licence to crenellate his manor house. The castle was owned by the abbey and was demolished in 1652.[83] Fragmentary masonry remains.

Notes

Chapter 1

1) 'unum Castrum dirutum vocatum Buckeden et nullius valoris', Harrop with Booth & Harrop 2005, xii-xiii, 14-5.
2) Brown 2004, 3 & 24' The 1954 edition gives a slightly different definition: "The private fortress and residence of a lord, whether king or baron", 1954, 17.
3) Liddiard 2005a, 36–38; Creighton 2002, 1; Goodall 2011, 4-6.
4) Higham 1991 lists five additional mottes for northern Lancashire and southern Cumbria based upon place-name and earthwork evidence.
5) Amongst the many castle studies painted by J M W Turner (1775-1851) were the Welsh sites of Conway, Caernarfon and Dolbadarn and in England Brougham, Dover, Kenilworth, Norham, Rochester and Windsor castles. John Constable (1776-1837) also sketched and painted castles including Arundle, Hadleigh, Old Sarum and Windsor. Moses Griffith (1747-1819), the Welsh engraver and water colourist, painted Chester Castle in the late 18th century before it was substantially altered.
6) Renn 1973; Brennand with Chitty & Nevell 2006, 140-43.
7) King 1983a & b.
8) Curwen 1913; Hugill 1977; Perriam & Robinson 1998.
9) Higham 1991; Salter 2001; Wood 1996.
10) Salter 2001.
11) Brown & Johnson 1985, 35-8; Battersby 2001; Tindall 1983, 5-8.
12) Droop 1928; Droop & Larkin 1928.
13) Perriam & Robinson 1998, 375.
14) Ellis 1993.
15) Lloyd Evans Prichard 2001; McCarthy *et al* 1990; Zant 2009; Perriam 1976.
16) Davey & McNeil 1980.
17) McNeil 1987.
18) Lewis 1999; Salter 2001, 33; Wood 1996, 143-4.
19) Newman 1987 & 1996; Summerson 1999, 33; Summerson, Trueman & Harrison 1998; Williams 1992.
20) LUAU 1995, 1997 & 1998; Turnbull & Walsh 1994.
21) Brennand with Chitty and Nevell 2006, 140-43.
22) Wood 1996, 145.
23) Cocroft 1996; Lowerre et al 2003.
24) Redhead 1997, 34-5; Dunham and Ullerwood were recorded in 1173 as being held against King Henry II.
25) Hartwell, Hyde & Pevsner 2004, 20; Morris 1983, 36-7; Redhead 1997.
26) Harrop with Booth & Harrop 2005; Nevell 1991, 115-7.
27) Higham 1991, 85; Wood 1996.
28) MacIvor 2001, 25.
29) Lott 1995; Brennand with Chitty & Nevell 2006, 141.
30) King 1983; Perriam & Robinson 1998. The first documentary reference to a castle is often not the date of its construction. Nor were all castles in the region recorded in the surviving medieval documents; this applies to most of the short-lived mottes of the North West. However even documentary references to stone castles are sometimes hard to find. The 1360 reference to Buckton Castle was not rediscovered until the 1970s.
31) Hyde & Pevsner 2010, 189, 340.

32) Hyde & Pevsner 2010, 192.
33) Hartwell with Pevsner 2009, 11; Salter 2001, 28-33.
34) King 1983; Champness 1992; Hartwell with Pevsner 2009, 11.
35) King 1983, 248; Pollard & Pevsner 2006, 19; Salter 2001, 34.
36) Hartwell, Hyde, Hubbard & Pevsner 2011, 247.
37) Lewis & Thacker 2005.
38) Hartwell, Hyde, Hubbard & Pevsner 2011, 566.
39) Hartwell, Hyde, Hubbard & Pevsner 2011, 566-7; McNeil 1987.
40) Ellis 1993; Hartwell, Hyde, Hubbard & Pevsner 2011, 127-8; Salter 2001, 12.
41) Hartwell, Hyde, Hubbard & Pevsner 2011, 584.
42) The garrison recorded at Burton-in-Lonsdale in 1129-30 included one knight, ten sergeants, a gatekeeper and a watchman. (Higham 1991, 79-90) Sometimes castles fell into royal hands, through confiscation or due to the minority of the new owner, leaving documents concerning their upkeep. Between 1316 and 1318, for instance, the Crown spent £363 on maintaining the garrisons at Appleby and Brougham castles on behalf of the Clifford family, at a time of war with Scotland (Perriam & Robinson 1998, 264-5; Summerson 1999, 4-5, 30-1). Other entries can be less helpful. The earliest documented reference to Buckton Castle comes in a set of accounts drawn up for the Black Prince who was then guardian of the lord of Longdendale in 1360. In these the castle was described as a ruin (Harrop with Booth & Harrop 2005). Other castles that came into royal hands, such as Chester, Carlisle and Lancaster, have left variable records concerning their building work and garrisoning.
43) Higham 1991.
44) Brennand with Chitty & Nevell 2006, 142
45) Perriam & Robinson 1998, 90, 348: Salter 1998.
46) Barrow 1994, 231-9; Oram 2008, 30-41.
47) Barrow 1994, 240-53; Oram 2008, 88-90.
48) Brennand with Chitty & Nevell 2006, 141; Higham 1991.
49) Coulson 1994 &2003; Creighton 2002; Johnson 2002; Liddiard 2005a.
50) Goodall 2011, 57-9.
51) Creighton 2002; Liddiard 2005b.
52) Higham 2004, 140-50
53) Brown 2004, 64.
54) Ellis 1993; Goodall 2011, 181-2.
55) Crosby 1998, 34-5; Goodall 2011, 181-3; Liddiard 2005a, 44.
56) Brown 2004, chapters 4 & 5.
57) Thompson 1987, 18.
58) Goodall 2011, 45-6.
59) Davies 2007, 228-233.
60) King 1988.
61) A licence to crenellate was granted to Lawrence of Ludlow, a wealthy wool merchant who had just purchased the manor, in 1291; Davies 2007.
62) Goodall 2011, 233-5.
63) Goodall 2011, 248-9.
64) Creighton 2002, 66-7; Goodall 2011, 217-21.
65) Creighton 2002, 75-8; Johnson 2002; Goodall 2011.
66) Coulson 2003; Liddiard 2005, 61-2.
67) Creighton 2002, 79-80; Goodall 2011, 314-7; Johnson 2002.
68) Summerson 1999.
69) Perriam & Robinson 1998, 90, 264; Summerson 1999.
70) Perriam & Robinson 2008, 388; Goodall 2011, 247.
71) Goodall 2011, 373; Perriam & Robinson 1998, 212
72) Davies 2007; King 1983a.

73) King 1983a; Davies 2007.
74) Oliver 2011, 47-56.
75) Arrowsmith 1995; Higham 1994, 150-4.
76) Wood 1996, 143.
77) Goodall 2011, 373-4.
78) Harrop with Booth & Harrop 2005; Arrowsmith 1997.
79) Ellis 1993c.
80) Extensive rebuilding in the early 19th century destroyed the greater part of the Medieval domestic ranges in the Outer Bailey at Chester, although it is likely that extensive below ground remains survive in this area; Ellis 1996; Ward 1993.
81) LUAU 1997.
82) King 1983b; Goodall 2011, 419-20.
83) Henry VIII stayed at Deal on several occasions; Coad 1998, 19-21; Goodall 2011, 419-23.
84) Brown 2004; King 1983a.
85) Perriam & Robinson 1998, 69-77; Summerson 2008, 31-3.
86) Brennand with Chitty & Nevell 2007, 107.
87) Brennand with Chitty & Nevell 2006, 142-3.

Chapter 2

1) Husain 1973, 83; Lewis 1991, 38-41.
2) Thacker 2005, 204.
3) Quoted by Alexander 1970, 715.
4) Lewis 1991, 42.
5) Husain 1973, 33 & Sawyer & Thacker 1987, 333-9. One of the reasons for the low Domesday value of the manors in Cheshire, and Lancashire 'between the Mersey and the Ribble', was the 'harrying of the north' by William I. The event saw the destruction of hundreds of manors in the early 1070s, as a punishment for the revolt of 1069-70. That revolt ended when William captured the last Saxon town to resist him – Chester (Higham 2004, 52-5, 142).
6) Husain 1973, 84-5.
7) Husain 1973, 85-8.
8) Barraclough 1988, ix-x.
9) Husain 1974, 88-90.
10) Oram 2008, 169, 186-7; Pounds 1990, 31; Stringer 1993, 17-22.
11) Husain 1973, 90.
12) Thacker 2005, 204.
13) Wareham 1995, 223.
14) Husain 1973, 90-1.
15) Nevell 2011, 45-7.
16) Husain 1973, 91-2.
17) Barraclough 1988, 294; Sanders 1963, 18.
18) Husain 1973, 91-4.
19) Husain 1973, 94.
20) Carpenter 1990, 326.
21) Husain 1973, 91-4.
22) Brown 1959, 262.
23) Brown 1959, 269, 280.
24) Brown 1959, 266, 269; King 1983a, 68.
25) Thompson 1966, 153-5.
26) Jenkins 1963, 11-5; English Heritage 2006, 8-9
27) Lewis 1991, 38-41.
28) Liddiard 2005, 18.

29) Jamieson 1987, 7.
30) King gave a density of one per every 44.1 miles, but taking Buckton and Watch Hill into account changes the figure. 1983a, 64.
31) King 1983a, 66.
32) King 1983a, 81; King 1983b, 489.
33) King 1983a, 132; King 1983b, 324, 419.
34) King 1983a, 201.
35) King 1983a, 64.
36) Goodall 2011, 9.
37) Davis 2006, 227-228.
38) Liddiard 2005, 43.
39) The licences refer to Doddington Tower (1364 and again in 1403), Macclesfield Castle (1398 and again in 1410), and Hooton Hall (1487). Davis 2006, 241-245.
40) Brown 1959, 269, 278.
41) Jamieson, Jones & Rodden 1987, 1.
42) Cited by Brown 1959, 278.
43) Jamieson, Jones & Rodden 1987, 1.
44) Burke & Nevell 1996, 16.
45) Grimsditch & Nevell 2011, 4 & 29.
46) Husain 1973, 33.
47) Creighton 2002, 35-6.
48) Liddiard 2005, 25.
49) Creighton 2002, 35.
50) Eales 2005, 19-20.
51) Nevell 1991, 10, 18; Nevell & Walker 1998, 48-51.
52) Nevell 1991, 96, 98.
53) Nevell 1991, 49-50.
54) King 1988, 62.
55) Nevell 1992, 83-4.
56) For a more detailed discussion of the cost of building the 10th-century keep of Château de Langeais in France in terms of labour see Bachrach 1984.
57) McNeill 2005, 33-4.
58) Brown 1955, 366; McNeill 2005, 36.
59) Eales 2005, fold out plan opposite 32.
60) Eales 2005, 23.
61) Brown 2004, 109; Painter 1943, 170-1.
62) Johnson & Fletcher 2011, 2; Nevell 1991, 115-6.
63) Keen 1993, 101.
64) The area of an oval is calculated by ($\pi \times r1 \times r2$) where r1 is half the length of the major axis, and r2 is half the length of the minor axis. The area of the walls was calculated by ($\pi \times 17.8 \times 13.1$) - ($\pi \times 15.0 \times 10.3$).
65) Grimsditch, Nevell & Redhead 2007, 44.
66) Eales 2005, 23.
67) For how to calculated the area of an oval see footnote 64. A 1991 estimate of the area of Buckton Castle being 0.35 ha (3,500m2) seems to be erroneous (Nevell 1991, 115).
68) Nevell 1991, 115.
69) Grimsditch, Nevell & Redhead 2007; Grimsditch & Nevell 2009.
70) Parnell 1993, 19-20.
71) Thompson 1966, 152-8.
72) Keen 1993, 100.
73) Thompson 1966, 158.
74) Thompson 1966, 155.

75) Initially it was thought that the made-up clay layer was deposited in the Tudor period, but the excavations led to a reassessment and it is now considered to date from the earliest phases of construction on the site. Thompson 1969, 216-7.
76) Thompson 1966, 154.
77) English Heritage, Scheduled Monument entry for Bolingbroke Castle http://list.english-heritage.org.uk/resultsingle.aspx?uid=1008318, accessed 1 June 2012.
78) Keen 1993, 100.
79) Ellis 1993a, 15.
80) Ellis 1993b, 109.
81) Thompson 1966, 155.
82) English Heritage, Scheduled Monument entry for Chartley Castle http://list.english-heritage.org.uk/resultsingle.aspx?uid=1011192, accessed 1 June 2012.
83) Lynam 1908, 353.
84) Mackenzie 1896, 392.
85) Salter 2001, 24–25.
86) Pettifer 1995, 134; Pettifer qualified his statement that the keep at Clitheroe was the smallest known by saying "reputedly".
87) Hartley & Newman 2006a, 14.
88) Hartley & Newman 2006b, 15.
89) King 1983a, 243-4.
90) Nevell 1991, 115.
91) Nevell 1991, 115.
92) Grimsditch & Nevell 2009, 35.
93) Alcock & King 1969, 106; Grimsditch & Nevell 2009, 35.
94) English Heritage, National Monuments Record Monument Type Thesaurus, hosted by the Gatehouse Gazetteer http://www.gatehouse-gazetteer.info/name2.html, accessed 1 June 2012.
95) Hull 2006, 97.
96) Pettifer 1995, 21.
97) Brown 2004, 56.
98) Brown 2004, 56.
99) Nevell 2010, 38-44.

Chapter 3

1) Roberts, Wilson & Nevell 2006, Shimwell 1998 and Tindall 1981. The fieldwork undertaken between 1995 and 2002 was led by John Roberts and Phil Wilson on behalf of the University of Manchester Archaeology Unit. This included the excavation in 1996 of four trenches over two banks to the north-west of the castle (Nevell & Walker 1998, 60-1), thought to be possibly an outer bailey (Nevell 1991, 116). This work revealed that these banks were mid-20th century features, with no medieval deposits or finds located in any of the trenches. The fieldwork undertaken in the period 1995-2002 was funded by Tameside MBC as part of the Tameside Archaeological Survey project
2) Grimsditch, Nevell & Redhead 2007; Grimsditch & Nevell 2009; Grimsditch & Nevell 2011. The 2007 to 2010 excavations were directed by Brian Grimsditch of the University of Salford (and formerly a member of the University of Manchester Archaeology Unit) with the support of Adam Thompson of the Centre for Applied Archaeology (CfAA) at the University of Salford, and John Roberts, formerly of the University of Manchester Archaeology Unit. The excavations were funded by Tameside MBC as part of the Tameside Archaeological Survey project. More than 60 adult volunteers took part in the project., along with four local archaeology societies and students from three universities.
3) Hodgson & Brennand 2006, 30-1; Tallis & McGuire 1972, 726; Tallis & Switsur 1973, 743.

4) Shimwell 1998.
5) Humphries 2008.
6) Grimsditch & Nevell 2009.
7) Grimsditch & Nevell 2011.
8) Tindall 1981, 19.
9) Grimsditch, Nevell & Redhead 2007.
10) Grimsditch & Nevell 2009.
11) Grimsditch & Nevell 2011.
12) Roberts, Wilson & Nevell 2006.
13) Structures (152) and (164) constituted the western and eastern walls respectively, and structures (160) and (167) forming the northern and southern walls.
14) The outer curtain wall was context (151) in Trench 2008/1.
15) Represented by deposit (158) in Trench 2008/3
16) Context (171) ion trench 2008/3.
17) The kerbstone were context 2008/3 (188) whilst the metalled surface was context (173).
18) The posthole is context 2008/3 (182).
19) The burnt layer was context 2008/3 (185).
20) Grimsditch & Nevell 2011.
21) Roberts, Wilson & Nevell 2006.
22) Roberts, Wilson & Nevell 2006.
23) Grimsditch, Nevell & Redhead 2007.
24) Grimsditch & Nevell 2010.
25) Grimsditch & Nevell 2011.
26) Grimsditch & Nevell 2010.
27) Nevell & Walker 1998a, 50-1; Nevell, Grimsditch & Redhead 2008.
28) Nevell 2011, 12.
29) Goodall 2011, 137-9.
30) Nevell 2011, 37, 51–52.
31) Brown 2004, 57; King 1988, 22.
32) Lynch 2001, 164; Oram 2008, 128-34, 169.
33) Brown 2004, 55-7; Creighton 2002, 199-202; Goodall 2011, 119-23; Oram 2008, 143-4; Stringer 1993, 17-22.
34) During the civil war and in its aftermath some 16 castles are known to have been slighted, as Buckton might have been. The majority of the slighted castles (11) were in the south, making the destruction of Buckton unusual, and most were demolished during the 1150s after the civil war (Nevell 2011, 22–29).
35) Chadwick 1870; Walker & Nevell 1998b.

Chapter 4

1) Harrop with Booth and Harrop 2005, entries 3.02 and 7.02; Public Record Office, Kew, Special Collections, Rentals, Surveys and Rolls; ref SC 11/897.
2) The Latin text for Membrane 3 reads as follows 'qui dicunt super sacramentum suum quod est ibi unum Castrum dirutum vocatum Buckeden'; Harrop with Booth and Harrop 2005, entries 3.02.
3) Andrew 1892, 54; Booth & Cronin 1989, 64.
4) Lancashire Record Office DDX 350/21.
5) Andrew 1903; Chetham's Library, Raines Mss ix, 141-2.
6) John Collier is better known as the Lancashire dialect poet 'Tim Bobbin'; the letter was preserved by Cannon Raines at the Chetham's Library, Raines Mss ix, 141-2; Earwaker 1880,174-5.
7) Chetham's Library, Raines Mss ix, 141-2.

8) The accounts of the steward of Lord Dysart are preserved in the Cheshire Record Office but begin a few years after the date of this letter. A search of these has revealed no mention of the finds, but there remains a possibility that some evidence may yet be found in the considerable body of other estate papers and letters held at Chester.
9) Andrew 1903, 9.
10) Manchester City Archives, GB127.MS 942.72 Pe10. There is some slight confusion over who Thomas Percival was. The manuscript in the Manchester City Archives is undated and the dates of his life are approximate. Aikin described him in 1795 as the 'late Thomas Percival Esq' but this seems as odds with the manuscript record (Aikin 1795, 471).
11) Nevell Walker 1998a, 60-1.
12) Watson 1777, 88. Watson read his paper to the Society of Antiquaries in London on May 3rd 1776.
13) Ormerod 1819, Volume III, 278-9.
14) Ormerod 1819, 279.
15) Farrer & Brownbill 1908, 516-7. Due to local government re-organisation in the 1890s Buckton was for a few years in the county of Lancashire.
16) Nevell 1993, 126-7; Nevell & Walker 2004, 28.
17) Nevell with Grimsditch & King 2006, 66-7.
18) Pers. comm. Ken Booth, Saddleworth Archaeology Society. The original is in the Saddleworth Heritage Centre.
19) Chetham's Library, Raines Mss ix, 141-2.
20) Andrew 1892, 54; Andrew 1895, 164-7.
21) Andrew 1892, 54-5.
22) Andrew 1895, 164-5.
23) Booth & Cronin 1989, 64-5.
24) Forde-Johnston 1962, 11-2. The idea that Buckton Castle may be a hillfort has persisted and as late as 1989 was mentioned as one possible origin of the site by Cronin & Booth (1989, 64).
25) Harrop with Booth & Harrop 2005; GMAU 1981.
26) Burke & Nevell 1996, 16.
27) Nevell & Walker 1998a, 60-1. A second possibility, although far less likely, is that Buckton Castle was built by an earl of Chester in response to the threat posed by the Peveril family. They were lords of northern Derbyshire, including Glossopdale which was the next major river valley to the south of Buckton. There is a tradition, recorded in the *Gesta Stephani*, that William Peveril II attempted to poison Ranulf II in 1153 (Eales 2006, 22). Buckton's location, however, is wrong if it was built to confront the Peverils, since it lies one valley too far to the north. A better position would have been further south in Mottram or Tintwistle facing Mouselow Castle, a motte which may have been built by the Peverils.
28) This was located by the Defence of Britain Survey in the 1990s at grid reference SD 997 017. However, this grid reference is a conversion from a military grid and may contain some inaccuracies. Buckton Castle lies close by at SD 9892 0162, and the concrete platform on the eastern side of the castle could represent the remains of the control room for the STARFISH site. The research for the Starfish site was undertaken with the assistance of Peter Leeming, formerly of the Greater Manchester Archaeology Unit.
29) Lowry 1995, 63-4.
30) Dobinson 1996, 144 & 149.

Chapter 5

1) Cathcart King 1983a, 68, 83; Perriam & Robinson 1998, 198.
2) Simpson 1982.

3) Summerson 2008, 23–31; English Heritage, English Heritage, Scheduled Monument entry for Carlisle Castle http://list.english-heritage.org.uk/resultsingle.aspx?uid=1014579, accessed 1 June 2012.
4) Thacker & Lewis 2003, 16–33; Thacker & Lewis 2005, 204–213.
5) Perriam & Robinson 1998, 252; English Heritage 2006, 8.
6) Ellis 1993.
7) Summerson, Trueman & Harrison 1998, 7–11, 13, 23.
8) English Heritage, Scheduled Monument entry for Greenhalgh Castle http://list.english-heritage.org.uk/resultsingle.aspx?uid=1013815, accessed 1 June 2012.
9) Champness 1993, 1, 3–6, 13.
10) Farrer & Bownbill 1911a, 4; Salter 2001, 34.
11) Perriam & Robinson 1998, 212; Perriam 2008.
12) Cathcart King 1983a, 68, 71; Revealing Cheshire's Past, Historic Environment Record for Shotwick Castle Motte and Bailey http://rcp.cheshire.gov.uk/SingleResult.aspx?uid=MCH1342, accessed 1 June 2012.
13) Shaw & Clark 2003a, 2, 8.
14) Davison 1969, 23–24; Higham 1991, 81.
15) Higham 1991, 83; Lancashire County Council, "Chapel Hill, Arkholme" http://www.lancashire.gov.uk/corporate/web/index.asp?siteid=4398&pageid=20345&e=e, retrieved 1 June 2012.
16) Cathcart King 1983a, 82; Perriam & Robinson 1998, 130.
17) Perriam & Robinson 1998, 59.
18) Cathcart King 1983a, 244.
19) Cathcart King 1983a, 82, 98; Perriam & Robinson 1998, 46.
20) Perriam & Robinson 1998, 137.
21) Farrer & Brownbill 1911b, 131; English Heritage, Scheduled Monument entry for Bury Castle http://list.english-heritage.org.uk/resultsingle.aspx?uid=1015128, accessed 1 June 2012.
22) Higham 1991, 88.
23) Higham 1991, 88; Lancashire County Council, "Castle Haugh" http://www.lancashire.gov.uk/corporate/web/index.asp?siteid=4398&pageid=20454&e=e, accessed 1 June 2012.
24) Higham 1991, 88; Lancashire County Council, "Castle Hill, Dolphinholme" http://www.lancashire.gov.uk/corporate/web/index.asp?siteid=4398&pageid=20348&e=e, accessed 1 June 2012.
25) Cathcart King 1983a, 250; English Heritage, Scheduled Monument entry for Clitheroe Castle http://list.english-heritage.org.uk/resultsingle.aspx?uid=1016196, accessed 1 June 2012; Hartley & Newman 2006a, 1; Farrer & Brownbill 1911c, 360–372.
26) Bradbury 1981, 39–40, 45.
27) Revealing Cheshire's History, Historic Environment Record for Dodlston Castle http://rcp.cheshire.gov.uk/SingleResult.aspx?uid=MCH1410, accessed 1 June 2012.
28) Perriam & Robinson 1998, 58.
29) Brown & Johnson 1985, 35; Cathcart King 1983a, 67.
30) Cathcart King 1983a, 86; Perriam & Robinson 1998, 102.
31) Revealing Cheshire's Past, Historic Environment Record for Frodsham Castle http://rcp.cheshire.gov.uk/SingleResult.aspx?uid=MCH7878, accessed 1 June 2012; Shaw & Clark 2003b, 5, 10–11.
32) Cathcart King 1983a, 245; English Heritage, Scheduled Monument entry for Gleaston Castle http://list.english-heritage.org.uk/resultsingle.aspx?uid=1013966, accessed 1 June 2012; Farrer & Brownbill 1914, 320–328; Perriam & Robinson 1998, 382.
33) Higham 1991, 88.
34) Devine & Clark 2003, 5-6.
35) Lancashire County Council, "Castle Hill, Halton" http://www.lancashire.gov.uk/corporate/web/index.asp?siteid=4398&pageid=20349&e=e, accessed 1 June 2012.

36) Cathcart King 1983a, 86;Perriam & Robinson 1998, 122.
37) Lyte 1907, 493; Perriam & Robinson 1998, 280.
38) Higham 1991, 88.
39) Cathcart King 1983a, 86; Lyte 1904, 82; Perriam & Robinson 1998, 104.
40) Jackson 1990, 60, referenced in Perriam & Robinson 1998, 155.
41) Cathcart King 1983a, 93, 100; Lyte 1900, 536.
42) Cathcart King 1983a, 246, 250; Hartley & Newman 2006b, 1, 8, 12.
43) Lancashire County Council, "Castle Stede" http://www.lancashire.gov.uk/corporate/web/index.asp?siteid=4398&pageid=20446&e=e, accessed 1 June 2012.
44) Cathcart King 1983a, 87; Perriam & Robinson 1998, 159.
45) Perriam & Robinson 1998, 335.
46) Perriam & Robinson 1998, 348.
47) Perriam & Robinson 1998, 336.
48) Cathcart King 1983a, 88; Perriam & Robinson 1998, 124.
49) Cathcart King 1983a, 88, 99.
50) Turner 1987, 136–138.
51) Shaw & Clark 2003c, 1, 8.
52) Nevell 2008, 41–42.
53) Perriam & Robinson 1998, 19.
54) Higham 1991, 83; Lancashire County Council, "Melling Motte" http://www.lancashire.gov.uk/corporate/web/index.asp?siteid=4398&pageid=20353&e=e, accessed 1 June 2012.
55) Lyte 1895, 167; Perriam & Robinson 1998, 115.
56) King 1983a, 249.
57) Shaw & Clark 2003d, 4-5.
58) Lyte 1895, 168; Perriam & Robinson 1998, 166.
59) Farrer & Brownbill 1908, 531-533.
60) Cathcart King 1983a, 69; Salter 2001, 20; Shaw & Clark 2003d.
61) Revealing Cheshire's Past, Historic Environment Record for Castle Hill, Oldcastle http://rcp.cheshire.gov.uk/SingleResult.aspx?uid=MCH1403, accessed 1 June 2012.
62) Cathcart King 1983b, 493, 496.
63) Farrer & Brownbill 1908, 556; Perriam & Robinson 1998, 388.
64) English Heritage, Scheduled Monument entry for Castle Hill Motte http://list.english-heritage.org.uk/resultsingle.aspx?uid=1011868; Harfield 1991, 383–384; Hartley & Newman 2006c, 21; Lancashire County Council, "Penwortham Castle" http://www.lancashire.gov.uk/corporate/web/index.asp?siteid=4398&pageid=20458&e=e, accessed 1 June 2012.
65) Cathcart King 1983a, 249, 251; Farrer & Brownbill 1908, 536-537.
66) Cathcart King 1983a, 68, 71.
67) Cathcart King 1983a, 247, 251; Farrer & Brownbill 1908, 537-538
68) Cathcart King 1983a, 69; Revealing Cheshire's Past, Historic Environment Record for Runcorn burh http://rcp.cheshire.gov.uk/SingleResult.aspx?uid=MCH5991, accessed 1 June 2012.
69) Lyte 1894, 8; Perriam & Robinson 1998,86.
70) Husain 1973, 99, 101.
71) Cathcart King 1983a, 68; Salter 2001, 21.
72) Arrowsmith 1997, 6, 31-32.
73) Perriam & Robinson 1998, 268, 279.
74) Cathcart King 1983a, 247; Lancashire County Council, "Thurland Castle" http://www.lancashire.gov.uk/corporate/web/index.asp?siteid=4398&pageid=20354&e=e, accessed 1 June 2012; Lyte 1905, 164.
75) Lyte 1898, 417; Perriam & Robinson 1998, 175.
76) Brown & Johnson 1985, 35.

77) Revealing Cheshire's Past, Historic Environment Record for Mote Hill http://rcp.cheshire.gov.uk/SingleResult.aspx?uid=MCH8625, accessed 1 June 2012.
78) Brown & Johnson 1985, 35; Redhead 1997, "Watch Hill Castle", 37.
79) Farrer & Brownbill 1908, 544; Farrer & Brownbill 1911a, 4.
80) Lancashire County Council, "Whittington Motte" http://www.lancashire.gov.uk/corporate/web/index.asp?siteid=4398&pageid=20356&e=e, accessed 1 June 2012.
81) Cathcart King 1983a, 247,251; Lyte 1891, 169; Perriam & Robinson 1998, 390.
82) Tatton-Brown 2004, 259-260.
83) Cathcart King 1983a, 91; Lyte 1906, 194; Perriam & Robinson 1998, 28.

Sources

Aikin J, 1795 *A Description of the Country Thirty to Forty Miles round Manchester*. London.

Alexander J W, 1970, "New Evidence on the Palatine of Cheshire". *The English Historical Review* **85**, 715-729.

Andrew S, 1892, 'Bucton', *Transactions of the Lancashire and Cheshire Antiquarian Society* **10**, 44-66.

Andrew S, 1895, 'Bucton Castle', *Transactions of the Lancashire and Cheshire Antiquarian Society* **13**, 164-7.

Andrew W J, 1903, 'Buried Treasure: some traditions, records and facts', *Journal of the British Archaeological Association, New Series* **9**, 8-32.

Arrowsmith P, 1995, *Radcliffe Tower - An Introduction to the Scheduled Ancient Monument*. Chester: Bury Metropolitan Borough Council.

Arrowsmith P, 1997, *Stockport, a History*. Stockport Metropolitan Borough Council with the University of Manchester Archaeological Unit.

Arrowsmith P, 1999, *Bury Castle - An Introduction to the Scheduled Ancient Monument*. Chester: Bury Metropolitan Borough Council.

Bachrach B S, 1984, "The Cost of Castle Building: The Case of the Tower of Langeais" in Reyerson K & Powe F (eds), *The Medieval Castle: Romance and Reality*. Minneapolis: University of Minnesota Press, 47-62.

Barraclough G (ed), 1988, *The Charters of the Anglo-Norman Earls of Chester c. 1071–1237*. Gloucester: Alan Sutton Publishing.

Barrow G W S, (ed.), 1994, *The Scottish Tradition*. Edinburgh.

Battersby Y, 2001, *Rochdale Castle, Castle Hill, Greater Manchester - Archaeological Evaluation*. Greater Manchester Archaeological Unit unpublished report.

Booth K, and Cronin J, 1989 'Buckton Castle: a survey of the evidence', *Greater Manchester Archaeological Journal 3* (for 1987-8), 61-6.

Brennand M, with Chitty J & Nevell M, (eds.), 2006, *The Archaeology of North West England: An Archaeological Research Framework for North West England. Vol 1: Resource Assessment*. ALGAO and English Heritage with the Council for British Archaeology North West.

Brennand M, with Chitty J & Nevell M, (eds.), 2007, *The Archaeology of North West England: An Archaeological Research Framework for North West England. Vol 2: Research Agenda and Strategy*. ALGAO and English Heritage with the Council for British Archaeology North West.

Bradbury B, 1981, *A History of Cockermouth*. London: Phillimore.

Brown K & Johnson B, 1985, 'Watch Hill, Bowdon', *Greater Manchester Archaeological Journal* **1**, 35-8.

Brown R A, 1955, "Royal Castle-Building in England, 1154–1216". *The English Historical Review* **70**, 19-64.

Brown R A, 1959, 'A List of Castles, 1154-1216', *English Historical Review* **74**, 249-80.

Brown R A, 2004, *Allen Brown's English Castles*. Woodbridge: The Boydell Press, third edition.

Burke T & Nevell M, 1996, *A History & Archaeology of Tameside, Volume 5: Buildings of Tameside*. Tameside Borough Council.

Carpenter D A, 1990, *The Minority of Henry III*. Berkeley: University of California Press.

Champness, J, 1993, *Lancaster Castle: A Brief History*. Preston: Lancashire County Books.
Chadwick W, 1870, *Reminiscences of Mottram*. Republished 1972 by Longdendale Amenity Society.
Cheshire Historic Towns Survey, 2003a, *Aldford: Archaeological Assessment*. Chester: Cheshire County Council and English Heritage.
Cheshire Historic Towns Survey, 2003b, *Aldford: Archaeological Strategy*. Chester: Cheshire County Council and English Heritage.
Coad J, 1998, *Deal Castle*. London: English Heritage.
Cocroft W, 1996, *Aldford Castle Cheshire, Report on geophysical survey*. Geophysical Surveys of Bradford, unpublished technical report no 96/05.
Coulson C, 1994, "The Castles of the Anarchy', in King E, (ed.), *The Anarchy of Stephen's Reign*. Oxford: Clarendon Press, 67-92.
Coulson C, 2003, 'Orthodoxy or Opportunity?', *Castle Studies Group Bulletin*, 115-6.
Creighton O, 2002, *Castles and Landscapes: Power, Community and Fortification in medieval England*. London: Equinox Publishing.
Creighton O & Higham R, 2003, *Medieval Castles*. Princes Risborough: Shire Archaeology.
Creighton O & Liddiard R, 2008, "Fighting Yesterday's Battle: Beyond War or Status in Castle Studies", *Medieval Archaeology* **52**, 161-9.
Crosby A, 1998, *A History of Lancashire*. Chichester: Phillimore.
Curwen J, 1913, *Castles and Towers of Cumberland and Westmorland, Westmorland, and Lancashire North-of-the-Sands Together with a Brief Historical Account of Border Warfare*. Cumberland and Westmorland Antiquarian and Archaeological Society. Extra Series Vol 13.

Davey P J & McNeil R, 1980, 'Excavations in South Castle Street, Liverpool 1976 and 1977', *Journal of the Merseyside Archaeology Society* **4**, 6-29.
Davis P, 2007, "English Licences to Crenellate 1199–1567", *Castle Studies Group Journal* **20**, 226-45.
Davison B K, 1969, 'Aldingham', *Current Archaeology* **2.1**, 23-4.
Devine V & Clark J, 2003, Cheshire *Historic Towns Survey: Runcorn & Halton Archaeological Assessment*. Chester: Cheshire County Council.
Dobinson C S, 1996, *Twentieth Century Fortifications in England, Volume III: Bombing Decoys of WWII, England's Passive Air Defence 1939-45*. York: Council for British Archaeology.
Donald Insall Associates Ltd, 2001, *Chester Castle Conservation Plan*. London: English Heritage.
Droop J P, 1928, 'Excavations at West Derby, Liverpool', *Antiquaries Journal* **8**, 40.
Droop J P & Larkin F C, 1928, 'Excavations at West Derby Castle', *Liverpool Annals of Archaeology & Anthropology* **15**, 47-55.

Eales R, 2005, *Peveril Castle*. London: English Heritage.
Earwaker J P, 1880 *East Cheshire: Past and Present*. London: Volume 2.
Ellis P, 1993a, "Introduction" in Ellis P (ed), *Beeston Castle, Cheshire: A Report on the Excavations 1968–85 by Laurence Keen and Peter Hough*. English Heritage Archaeological report 23. London: English Heritage, 13-18.
Ellis P, 1993b, "The excavations" in Ellis P (ed), *Beeston Castle, Cheshire: A Report on the Excavations 1968–85 by Laurence Keen and Peter Hough*. English Heritage Archaeological Report 23. London: English Heritage, 108-131.
Ellis P, (ed.), 1993s, *Beeston Castle, Cheshire: Excavations by Laurence Keen and Peter Hough,*

1968-85. London: English Heritage Archaeological Report 23.

Ellis P, (ed.), 1996, *Excavations at Chester, Chester Castle, the seventeenth-century armoury and mint*. Chester Archaeology excavation and survey report 10. Chester City Council.

English Heritage, 2006, *Extensive Urban Survey – Cumbria*. Cumbria County Council.

Farrer W & Brownbill J, (eds), 1908, *A History of the County of Lancaster: Volume 2*. London: Victoria County History.

Farrer W & Brownbill J, (eds), 1911a, *A History of the County of Lancaster: Volume 4*. London: Victoria County History.

Farrer W & Brownbill J, (eds), 1911b, *A History of the County of Lancaster: Volume 5*. London: Victoria County History.

Farrer W & Brownbill J, (eds), 1911c, *A History of the County of Lancaster: Volume 6*. London: Victoria County History.

Farrer W & Brownbill J, (eds), 1912, *A History of the County of Lancaster: Volume 7*. London: Victoria County History.

Farrer W & Brownbill J, (eds), 1914, *A History of the County of Lancaster: Volume 8*. London: Victoria County History.

Forde-Johnston J, 1962, 'The Iron age Hillforts of Lancashire and Cheshire', *Transactions of Lancashire & Cheshire Antiquarian Society* **72**, 9-46.

Goodall J, 2011, *The English Castle, 1066-1650*. London: Yale University Press.

Grimsditch B & Nevell M, 2009, *Buckton Castle Tameside: A Report on the Second Season Archaeological Excavations by the University of Manchester*. CfAA Report No. 1, unpublished client report, University of Salford.

Grimsditch B & Nevell M, 2011, *Buckton Castle, Tameside: A Report on the Third Season of Archaeological Excavations*. Unpublished client report, Centre for Applied Archaeology, University of Salford.

Grimsditch B, Nevell M & Redhead N, 2007, *Buckton Castle: An Archaeological Evaluation of a Medieval Ringwork – An Interim Report*. Unpublished excavation report by University of Manchester Archaeological Unit.

Harfield C G, 1991, 'A Hand List of Castles Recorded in the Domesday Book', *English Historical Review* 106, 371-92.

Harrop J with Booth P and Booth S, 2005, *Extent of the Lordship of Longdendale, 1360*. Record Society of Lancashire and Cheshire, volume 140.

Hartwell C, Hyde M, Hubbard E & Pevsner N, 2011, *The Buildings of England. Cheshire*. London & New York: Yale University Press.

Hartwell C, Hyde M & Pevsner N, 2004, *The Buildings of England. Lancashire: Manchester and the South-East*. London & New York: Yale University Press.

Hartley S & Newman R, 2006a, *Lancashire Historic Towns Survey Programme: Clitheroe Historic Town Assessment Report*. Preston: Lancashire County Council.

Hartley S & Newman R, 2006b, *Lancashire Historic Towns Survey Programme: Hornby Historic Town Assessment Report*. Preston: Lancashire County Council.

Hartley S & Newman R, 2006c, *Lancashire Historic Towns Survey Programme: Preston Historic Town Assessment Report*. Preston: Lancashire County Council.

Hartwell C & Pevsner N, 2009, *The Buildings of England: Lancashire: North*. London & New York: Yale University Press. Second edition.

Higham M C, 1991, 'The mottes of North Lancashire, Lonsdale and South Cumbria',

Transactions of the Cumberland & Westmorland Antiquarian & Archaeological Society (New Series) **91**, 79-90.

Higham N J, 2004, *A Frontier Landscape: The North-West in the Middle Ages*. Macclesfield: Windgather Press.

Higham R & Barker P, 1994, *Timber Castles*. London: B T Batsford.

Hodgson J & Brennand M, 2006, 'Prehistoric Resource Assessment', in Brenannd with Chitty & Nevell, 23-58.

Hough P, 1978, "Excavations at Beeston Castle", *Journal of the Chester Archaeological Society* **61**, 1-24.

Hugill R, 1977, *Castles and Peles of Cumberland and Westmorland*. Newcastle: Frank Graham.

Hull L, 2006, *Britain's Medieval Castles*. Westport: Praeger Publishers.

Humphries P, 2008, *On the Trail of Turner in North and South Wales*. Cardiff: Cadw. Third edition.

Husain B M C, 1973, *Cheshire under the Norman Earls, 1066-1237*. Chester: Cheshire Community Council Publications Trust.

Hyde M & Pevsner N, 2010, *The Buildings of England. Cumbria: Cumberland, Westmorland and Furness*. London & New York: Yale University Press.

Jackson M J, 1990, *Castles of Cumbria*. Carlisle: Carel Press.

Jamieson A, 1987, "Building Records to 1738" in McNeil R & Jamieson A (eds), *Halton Castle – 'A Visual Treasure'*. Liverpool: North West Archaeological Trust, 7.

Jamieson A, Jones J & Rodden P, 1987, "Historical Background" in McNeil R & Jamieson A (eds), *Halton Castle – 'A Visual Treasure'*. Liverpool: North West Archaeological Trust. 1-6.

Jenkins J, 1963, "Newcastle-under-Lyme: Buildings and Castle" in Jenkins J (ed), *A History of the County of Stafford: Volume 8,* 8-15.

Johnson, C & Fletcher M, 2011, *Strategic Stone Study: A Building Stone Atlas of Greater Manchester*. London: English Heritage.

Johnson M, 2002, *Behind the Castle Gate*. London: Routledge.

Keen L, 1993, "The castle: history and structure" in Ellis P (ed), *Beeston Castle, Cheshire: A Report on the Excavations 1968–85 by Laurence Keen and Peter Hough*. English Heritage Archaeological Report 23. London: English Heritage, 93-107.

Kendrick J, 1853, 'An account of excavations made at the Mote Hill, Warrington, Lancashire', *Transactions of the Historic Society of Lancashire & Cheshire* **5**, 59-68.

King D J C, 1983a, *Castellarium Anglicanum: An Index and Bibliography of the Castles in England, Wales and the Islands. Vol.1, Anglesey-Montgomery*. London: Kraus International.

King D J C, 1983b, *Castellarium Anglicanum: An Index and Bibliography of the Castles in England, Wales and the Islands. Vol.2, Norfolk-Yorkshire and the Islands*. London: Kraus International.

King D J C, 1988, *The Castle in England and Wales: An Interpretative History*. London: Croom Helm.

King D J C, & Alcock L, 1969, "Ringworks of England and Wales", *Château Gaillard* **III**, 90-127.

Lewis C P, 1991, "The Formation of the Honour of Chester, 1066–1100". *Journal of the Chester Archaeological Society* **71**, 37-68.

Lewis J M, 1999, "Lathom House: The Northern Court", *Journal of the British Archaeological Association* **CLII**, 150-71.

Lewis J M, 2000, *The Medieval Earthworks of the Hundred of West Derby: Tenurial Evidence and Physical Structure*. Oxford: British Archaeological Reports (British Series) 310.

Lewis J M & Cowell R, 2002, *The Archaeology of a Changing Landscape. The Last Thousand Years in Merseyside*. Journal of the Merseyside Archaeology Society **11**.

Liddiard R, 2005a, *Castles in Context: Power, Symbolism and Landscape, 1066 to 1500*. Macclesfield: Windgather Press.

LiddiardR, 2005b, "Review of Castle and Landscapes", *Medieval Archaeology* **49**, 519-20.

Lloyd Evans Prichard, 2001, *Carlisle Castle Conservation Plan*. 2 volumes. Unpublished client report.

Lott B, 1995, *Medieval Buildings in Westmorland*. Unpublished PhD thesis, University of Nottingham.

Lowerre A, 2003, *Aldford Castle, Cheshire, 2002 Excavation interim report*. Chester Archaeology evaluation report 66, unpublished report.

Lowry B, 1995, *Twentieth-century Defences in Britain: An Introductory Guide. CBA Practical Handbooks in Archaeology, No 12*. York: Council for British Archaeology.

LUAU, 1995, *Lancaster Castle Gatehouse, Lancashire. Archaeological Watching Brief and Excavation*. Lancaster University Archaeological Unit unpublished report.

LUAU, 1997, *Lancaster Castle, Lancashire. Archaeological Intervention Works on the Witches' Tower Upper Floor*. Lancaster University Archaeological Unit unpublished report.

LUAU, 1998, *Egremont Castle Revetment Walls, Egremont, Cumbria: Watching Brief*. Lancaster University Archaeological Unit

Lynam C, 1908, "Ancient Earthworks" in Page W (ed), *A History of the County of Stafford: Volume 1,* 332-79.

Lynch M, 2001, *The Oxford Companion to Scottish History*. Oxford.

Lyte H C M (ed), 1891, *Calendar of Patent Rolls (1327–30)*. London: HMSO.

Lyte H C M (ed), 1894, *Calendar of Patent Rolls (1307–13)*. London: HMSO.

Lyte H C M (ed), 1895, *Calendar of Patent Rolls (1334–38)*. London: HMSO.

Lyte H C M (ed), 1898, *Calendar of Patent Rolls (1338–40)*. London: HMSO.

Lyte H C M (ed), 1900, *Calendar of Patent Rolls (1340–43)*. London: HMSO.

Lyte H C M (ed), 1904, *Calendar of Patent Rolls (1321–24)*. London: HMSO.

Lyte H C M (ed), 1905, *Calendar of Patent Rolls (1401–05)*. London: HMSO.

Lyte H C M (ed), 1906, *Calendar of Patent Rolls (1348–50)*. London: HMSO.

Lyte H C M (ed), 1907, *Calendar of Patent Rolls (1350–54)*. London: HMSO.

MacIvor I, 2001, *A Fortified Frontier: Defences of the Anglo-Scottish Border*. Stroud: Tempus.

Mackenzie J D, 1896, *Castles of England. Volume 1*. New York: Macmillan.

McNeil R, 1987, *Halton Castle: A Visual Treasure*. Liverpool, North West Archaeological Trust, Report 1.

McNeill T, 2005, *Castles*. London: English Heritage, second edition.

McCarthy M R, Summerson H R T & Annis R G, 1990, *Carlisle Castle. A Survey and Documentary History*. London, English Heritage Archaeological Report 18.

Morris, M., (ed.), 1983, *Medieval Manchester: A Regional Study*. The Archaeology of Greater Manchester volume 1.

Nevell M, 1991, *A History and Archaeology of Tameside, Volume 2. Tameside, 1066–1700*. Tameside Metropolitan Borough Council.

Nevell M, 1992, *A History and Archaeology of Tameside, Volume 1. Tameside Before 1066.* Tameside Metropolitan Borough Council.

Nevell M, 1993, *A History and Archaeology of Tameside, Volume 3: Tameside 1700-1930,* Tameside Metropolitan Borough Council.

Nevell M, 2008, *Manchester: The Hidden History.* Stroud: The History Press.

Nevell M, Grimsditch B & Redhead N, 2008, 'Buckton Castle', *Current Archaeology* **19.9**, 32-37.

Nevell M & Walker J, 1998, *A History and Archaeology of Tameside, Volume 6. Lands and Lordships in Tameside: Tameside in Transition 1348 to 1642.* Tameside Metropolitan Borough Council.

Nevell M & Walker J, 2004 *A History and Archaeology of Tameside Volume 8: The Archaeology of Twentieth Century Tameside. From Lordship to Local Authority. The Archaeology of the Later Industrial Period, 1870-2000.* Michael Nevell & John Walker. Tameside MBC with UMAU.

Nevell R, 2010, *In the Shadow of the Gatehouse: A study of castle gates and approaches in North West England.* unpublished BA dissertation, University of Leicester.

Nevell R, 2011, *King of the Castle: A study of castle slighting in the 12th and 13th centuries.* unpublished MA dissertation, University of Leicester.

Newman C, 2006, 'The Medieval Period Resource Assessment', in Brennand M with Chitty J & Nevell M, (eds), *The Archaeology of North West England: An Archaeological Research Framework for North West England. Volume 1. Resource Assessment.* Council for British Archaeology North West, 115-44.

Newman C & Newman R, 2007, 'The Medieval Period Research Agenda'. in Brennand M with Chitty J & Nevell M, (eds), *Research and Archaeology in North West England: An Archaeological Research Framework for North West England. Volume 2. Research Agenda and Strategy.* Council for British Archaeology North West, 95-114.

Newman R M, 1987, 'Excavations and Survey at Piel Castle, near Barrow-in-Furness, Cumbria', *Transactions of the Cumberland & Westmorland Antiquarian & Archaeology Society (New Series)* **87**, 101-16.

Newman R M, 1996, 'Further Structural Analysis at Piel Castle, 1987-94', *Transactions of the Cumberland & Westmorland Antiquarian & Archaeology Society (New Series)* **96**, 121-37.

Newman R, 1996, *The Archaeology of Lancashire: Present State and Future Priorities.* Lancaster, Lancaster University Archaeological Unit.

Oliver N, 2009, *A History of Scotland.* London: Weidenfield & Nicolson.

Ormerod G, (ed.), 1819 *The History of the County Palatine and City of Chester.* Second edition, enlarged and revised by T Helsby in 1882, volume III.

Oram R, 2008, *David I: The King Who Made Scotland.* Stroud: History Press.

Penney, S. 1981. *Lancaster: The Evolution of its Townscape to 1800.* Lancaster: Centre for North West Regional Studies, University of Lancaster.

Perriam D R, 1976, 'The demolition of Carlisle city walls', *Transactions of the Cumberland & Westmorland Antiquarian & Archaeology Society (New Series)* **76**, 184-98.

Perriam D R, 2008, "William Strickland's tower in Penrith: Penrith Castle or Hutton Hall?", *English Heritage Historical Review* 3, 36-45.

Perriam D R & Robinson J, 1998, *The Medieval Fortified Buildings of Cumbria.* Cumberland and Westmorland Antiquarian and Archaeological Society Extra Series 29.

Pevsner N & Hubbard E, 1971, *The Buildings of England: Cheshire.* Penguin Books.

Painter S, 1943, *Studies in the history of the English feudal barony*. Baltimore: The John Hopkins Press.
Parnell G, 1993, *The Tower of London*. London: English Heritage.
Pettifer A, 1995, *English Castles: A Guide by Counties*. Woodbridge: The Boydell Press.
Platt C, 2006, "Review of The Idea of the Castle", *Medieval Archaeology* **50**, 404-5.
Platt C, 2007, "Revisionism in Castle Studies: A Caution", *Medieval Archaeology* **51**, 83-102.
Pollard R & Pevsner N, 2006, *The Buildings of England. Lancashire: Liverpool and the South-West*. London: Yale University Press.
Pounds N, 1990, *The Medieval Castle in England and Wales: A Social and Political History*. Cambridge: Cambridge University Press.

Redhead N, 1997, 'Watch Hill Castle', in Nevell M, 1997, 34-5.
Renn D F, 1973, *Norman Castles in Britain*. London: Humanities Press, second edition.
Richardson A, 2006,,"Review of Castles in Context", *Medieval Archaeology* **50**, 405-7.
Roberts J, Wilson P & Nevell M, 2006, *Buckton Castle, Stalybridge, Tameside. Archaeological Survey and Excavation Work by the University of Manchester Archaeological Unit 1996 to 2002*. University of Manchester Archaeology Unit, unpublished client report.

Salter M, 1998, *The Castles and Tower Houses of Cumbria*. Malvern: Folly Publications.
Salter M, 2001, *The Castles and Tower Houses of Lancashire and Cheshire*. Malvern: Folly Publications.
Sanders I J, 1963, *English Baronies: a study of their origin and descent, 1086–1327*. Wotton-under-Edge: Clarendon Press.
Shaw M & Clark J, 2003a, *Cheshire Historic Towns Survey: Aldford Archaeological Assessment*. Chester: Cheshire County Council.
Shaw M & Clark J, 2003b, *Cheshire Historic Towns Survey: Frodsham Archaeological Assessment*. Chester: Cheshire County Council.
Shaw M & Clark J, 2003c, *Cheshire Historic Towns Survey: Malpas Archaeological Assessment*. Chester: Cheshire County Council.
Shaw M & Clark J, 2003d, *Cheshire Historic Towns Survey: Nantwich Archaeological Assessment*. Chester: Cheshire County Council.
Shaw M & Clark J, 2003e, *Cheshire Historic Towns Survey: Northwich Archaeological Assessment*. Chester: Cheshire County Council.
Shimwell D W, 1998, *Preliminary Report on Three Environmental Context Samples from Buckton C-Castle, Tameside, Greater Manchester*. Unpublished research report, Palaeo-Environmental Research Unit, University of Manchester.
Simpson W D, 1982, *Brough Castle. Westmorland*. London: HMSO.
Stretton E H A, 1994, *Dacre Castle*. Penrith.
Stringer K J, 1993, *The Reign of Stephen. Kingship, Warfare and Governement in Twelfth-Century England*. London & New York: Routledge.
Summerson H, Trueman M & Harrison S, 1998, *Brougham Castle, Cumbria*. Cumberland & Westmorland Antiquarian & Archaeological Society Research Series Number 8.
Summerson H 1999, *Brougham and Brough Castles*. London: English Heritage.
Summerson H, 2008, *Carlisle Castle*. London: English Heritage.
Summerson H; Trueman M & Harrison S, 1998, *Brougham Castle Cumbria: A Survey and Documentary History*. Kendal: The Cumberland & Westmorland Antiquarian & Archaeological Society.

Tallis J H & McGuire J, 1972, 'Central Rossendale: the Evolution of an Upland Vegetation', *Journal of Ecology* **60**, 721-51.

Tallis J H & Switsur VR, 1973, 'Studies on southern Pennine peats VI. A radio-carbon dated pollen diagram from Featherbed Moss, Derbyshire', *Journal of Ecology* **61**, 743-51.

Tatton-Brown T, 2004, "Rose Castle" in McCarthy, Mike and Weston David (eds.) *Carlisle and Cumbria: Roman and Medieval Architecture, Art and Archaeology*. The British Archaeological Association Conference Transactions XXVII.

Taylor C, Everson P & Wilson-North R, 1990, "Bodiam Castle, Sussex", *Medieval Archaeology* **34**, 155-7.

Thompson M, 1994, "The Military Interpretation of Castles", *Archaeological Journal* **151**, 439-45.

Thackray D, 1991, *Bodiam Castle*. London: National Trust.

Thacker A T & Harris B E (eds.), 1987, *A History of the County of Cheshire: Volume 1*. London: Victoria County History.

Thacker A T & Lewis C P (eds.), 2003, *A History of the County of Cheshire: Volume 5 Part 1: The City of Chester: General History and Topography*. London: Victoria County History.

Thacker A T & Lewis C P (eds.), 2005, *A History of the County of Cheshire: Volume 5 Part 2: The City of Chester: Culture, Buildings, Institutions*. London: Victoria County History.

Thacker A T, 2005, "Chester: Castle" in Thacker A T & Lewis C P (eds.), *A History of the County of Chester: Volume 5 Part 2*. London: Victoria County History, 204-213.

Thompson M W, 1966, "The origins of Bolingbroke Castle Lincolnshire", *Medieval Archaeology* **10**, 152-8.

Thompson M W, 1969, "Further work at Bolingbroke Castle Lincolnshire", *Medieval Archaeology* **13**, 216-7.

Thompson M W, 1987, *The Decline of the Castle*. Cambridge University Press.

Tindall A, 1981, *Buckton Castle, Mossley*. Greater Manchester Archaeological Unit unpublished technical report.

Turnbull P & Walsh D, 1994, 'Recent work at Egremont castle', *Transactions of the Cumberland & Westmorland Antiquarian & Archaeological Society (Second Series)* **94**, 77-89.

Turner R C, 1987, "Macclesfield Castle", *Transactions of the Ancient Monuments Society* **31**, 134-45.

Walker J & Nevell M, 1998, *The Folklore of Tameside: Myths and Legends*. Tameside Metropolitan Borough with the University of Manchester Archaeological Unit.

Ward S W, 1993, *Chester Castle, Chester; an Archaeological Evaluation. Archaeological Service*. Evaluation Report 20. Chester, Chester City Council unpublished evaluation report.

Wareham A, 1995, "The Motives and Politics of the Bigod Family, c.1066–1177", *Anglo-Norman Studies* **17**, 223-242.

Watson Rev J, 1777, 'An Account of some hitherto undescribed Remains of Antiquity', *Archaeologia* **5**, 87-94.

Williams J H, 1992, 'Excavations at Brougham Castle, 1987', *Transactions of the Cumberland & Westmorland Antiquarian & Archaeology Society (New Series)* **87**, 105-21.

Wood J, 1996, 'Castles and monasteries', in Newman R, (ed), 1996, 139-56.

Zant J M, 2009, *Carlisle Millennium Project – Excavations in Carlisle 1998-2001: Stratigraphy. Volume 1*. Lancaster: Oxford Archaeology North.

Glossary of Terms

Apse A semi-circular end of a building.

Ashlar Masonry of large blocks finished with even faces and square edges.

Bailey A courtyard in a castle.

Barbican An outer fortification in front of the gate of a castle.

Buttress Vertical projection from a wall to stabilize it or to resist the lateral thrust of an arch, roof or vault.

Causeway A raised roadway crossing a castle ditch.

Crenellate / Crenellation Battlements at the top of the curtain wall, tower or keep, where the solid sections (merlons) shielded the defenders and the gaps (crenels) from which they could fire at the enemy.

Curtain Wall The wall around the perimeter of a castle or one of its courtyards.

Garderobe A medieval privy.

Gatehouse The building housing the entrance to a courtyard.

Gatepassage the routeway through the gatehouse.

Hall The room in the castle reserved for the public life of the lord, courts and solemn feasts.

Honour A large collection of lands held by a lord.

Keep A 16th century term for the medieval great tower.

Machicolations A line of stone projecting from the top of a wall. An outer wall is carried on these stones, between which were holes through which defenders can drop stones on to the base o the wall below.

Metalled / Metalling a rough stone surface of a path or roadway.

Motte A large, normally round, flat-topped, mound of earth which supported a tower or other building.

Palatine Princely levels of power and autonomy given by the king to a leading medieval noble, in a frontier area.

Portcullis A wooden grille which could be raised or lowered in grooves on either side of a gate passage to act as a gate.

Rampart A wall, especially one of earth, with a walkway on top. Usually found behind the castle ditch.

Slighting The deliberate damage of a fortification outside the context of battle. This was particularly common in periods of civil unrest.

Tower House Small castle consisting mainly or entirely of a single tower.

Undercroft Ground or cellar storage in building, keep or tower, that was vaulted.

Ward Courtyard in a castle.

Acknowledgements

The 2007 to 2010 excavations were directed by Brian Grimsditch of the University of Salford with the support of Adam Thompson of the Centre for Applied Archaeology (CfAA) at the University of Salford, and John Roberts, formerly of the University of Manchester Archaeology Unit (UMAU). Other staff involved in the project were Stephen Bell, Matt Bishop, Sarah Cattell, Ruth Garratt, Phil Cooke, Lee Gregory, Graham Mottershead, and Vicky Nash who worked in frequently adverse weather conditions with wit and good humour.

Thanks are due to the many people who assisted in the 2007 to 2010 excavations seasons. Steve Milne, Kevin Wright, Dave Barker and other members of the Tameside Archaeological Society (TAS); Derek Pierce, Ron Bragg, Brian Burton, Richard Nevell and other members of the South Trafford Archaeology Group; Andy Coutts of the South Manchester Archaeological Research Team (SMART); Lorraine Gregory and other members of the Glossop and Longdendale Historical Society; undergraduate and graduate archaeology students from the Universities of Leicester, Manchester and Salford; and to the more than 60 volunteers who participated in the three digs.

Thanks are also due to Norman Redhead County Archaeologist for Greater Manchester at GMAU, and latterly head of the Greater Manchester Archaeological Advisory Service whose assistance before, during, and after the fieldwork, and suggestions as to the form of the final publication, were invaluable. Gordon Dick and Stuart Sharp, managers of the Buckton Vale Quarry (Bardon Aggregates), granted permission for the use of the quarry car park, location of dig facilities and access to the castle via the quarry road system. Enville Estates, the agents for the landowners of the Buckton Castle site, gave their permission to access the site. Thanks are also due to Andrew Davidson of English Heritage, for his support and professional advice.

The fieldwork undertaken between 1995 and 2002 was led by John Roberts and Phil Wilson on behalf of UMAU with the assistance of Tony Anderson, Jane Berry, Graham Eyre-Morgan, Stacey Hallett, Carolanne King, Robina McNeil, Catherine Parker, Catherine Pickles, and Lynne Walker. Topographical survey work was undertaken by Tom Burke, David Lloyd, Keith Maude and David Power. Peter Arrowsmith, Michael Nevell and John Walker (former Director of UMAU) undertook the documentary research and report writing during this period.

Thanks are also due for assistance given during the production of the current book. Peter Leeming provided advice on the use of Buckton Castle in the post-medieval period, Carla Brain helped with the proof reading, and Catherine Mackey provided editorial assistance. Greg Colley of Suave Aerial Photographers, took aerial photographs of the castle during the 2010 excavations (http://www.suaveairphotos.co.uk/) and allowed use of this material for the current publication.

Finally, thanks also go to Tameside Metropolitan Borough Council for their support and funding of the investigation, and to the late Roy Oldham (1934-2010), leader of Tameside Metropolitan Borough Council from 1980 until 2010, for his personal vision, support, and enthusiasm for the project.

The publication of this monograph marks the completion of the Tameside Archaeology Survey, a landscape project that began in 1990, was funded by Tameside MBC, and was directed throughout by Michael Nevell. The authors have had the privilege to work on one of the longest-running archaeological projects in North West England. Over 22 years it has made a significant impact on the understanding of the archaeology and history of the region through numerous articles, 110 historic building surveys, 30 research excavations and 18 books. Its national impact can be seen in the six awards the project won, and in the adoption by researchers of the 'Manchester Methodology', an approach to charting archaeologically the impact of industrialisation on local communities.

Brian Grimsditch, Michael Nevell & Richard Nevell
CfAA, University of Salford, July 2012

Index

Entries in red indicate pages on which figures and their captions occur

A

Aikin, John antiquary 92
Aldford Castle 7, 14, 16, 19, 104
Aldingham Castle 5, 104
Aln, river 26
Altrincham 5
Appleby Castle 10, 14, 17, 19, 39, 101
Arkholme Castle 14, 19, 104, 110
Ashton 29
Askham Hall 19
Askerton Castle 105

B

Barrow 26
Beaumaris Castle 21
Beaumont Castle 19, 105
Beeston Castle 5, 6, 7-8, 11, 13-4, 19, 30, 37, 38, 40, 42, 45, 48, 50, 51, 53, 101-2
Berkley Castle 49
Berkshire 54
Bewcastle 18-19, 105
Bewley Castle 19
Blackburn 52
Blackrod Castle 7, 105
Bodiam castle 24-6, 27
Bolingbroke Castle 19, 37-8, 48-51, 53
Bollin, River 7, 14
Borwick 15
Bowdon 14
Brampton Castle 105
Bridgnorth 38
Brown, Allen, castle historian 1, 19, 38, 44
Brough Castle 5, 9, 10, 14, 17, 18, 26, 31, 99, 101

Brougham Castle 5, 9-10, 14, 17, 19, 26, 102
Buck, Nathaniel & Samuel, artists 3, 101
Buckton Castle 1, 5-7, 14, 29, 33, 35, 37, 41-97, 102
  beacons 87
  curtain wall 65-70
  ditch 62-5
  excavations, 58-85
  gatehouse 70-6
  historic plans 91
  interior 76-9
  pre-castle landscape 60-1
  quarry 60
  Second World War decoy site 95-7
  smallfinds 80-1
  treasure 87-90
Buckton Vale Print Works 92-3
Bury Castle 19, 29, 105-6
Butterworth, James, historian 92

C

Caernarfon Castle 21, 24
Camber Castle 30
Carlisle Castle 5, 10, 11, 17-9, 30-1, 32, 36, 84, 100
Castle Banks 106
Castle Carrock 19
Castle Haugh 106
Castle Hill 106
Castles
  chapels 19
  distribution 4
  early 2, 7-9
  keeps 10
  stone 9-14
  timber 2
Castlestede, Hornby 108-9
Castleton (Church Shocklach) 7
Carrbrook 92-3
Chartley Castle 11, 38, 48, 51

Cheetham College 5
Chepstow Castle 43
Chester 1, 2,14, 18, 35-6, 39, 55
  castle vi, 3, 5, 7, 11, 13, 19, 30, 37, 100-1
  earls of 11, 19, 35-9, 42, 47-8, 51-3, 55, 81-5, 100, 104, 110
Cheshire 1, 2, 5, 7, 11, 13-4, 16, 19, 29, 35, 38-43, 83, 85, 92, 94, 98, 100-1, 104, 106, 108, 110-2, 114-5
Clitheroe Castle 10, 12, 17, 30, 46, 50, 51, 52, 98, 106
Clifford family 26, 31, 99-100, 102
Cockermouth 26, 106
Constable, John, artist 3
Constantinople 19-20
Conwy 24
Corfe Castle 43
Cumbria 3, 5, 6, 8-9, 15, 19, 26, 29, 31, 99-102, 104-14
Cumberland 41-2, 85

D

David, king of Scotland 81, 84-5, 100
Deal Castle, Kent 30
Dee, river and valley 14, 16, 36, 104
Degannwy Castle 38
Denbighshire 15, 38
Derbyshire 42-3
Dodleston Castle 7, 19, 106
Doddington 29, 40
Domesday Book 15, 35, 39, 43
Dover Castle 19
Down Hall 106
Dunham Castle 7, 19, 38, 106, 114
Durham
  castle 41-2, 54
  Treaty of 17, 85

Dunstanburgh Castle 22-3, 24

E

Eden, river and valley 10, 14, 26
Edward I, king of England 15, 21, 24, 99-101, 104
Edward II, king of England 99, 103
Edward III, king of England 23
Egremont Castle 6, 9, 107
Ellenthorpe 17
England 1, 14, 47
Essex 2
Exeter 18

F

Farnham Castle 54
Flintshire 15, 38, 41
Frodsham Castle 40-1, 107
Furness 114

G

Gisburn 17
Gleaston Castle 107
Glossopdale 45
Greater Manchester 5-7, 102, 105, 112-4
Greenhalgh Castle 29, 102
Griffith, Moses, artist 3

H

Hadrian's Wall 18, 105
Hall Hill 108
Halton Castle, Lancashire 8, 108
Halton Castle, Cheshire 5, 12, 30, 42, 108
Haresceugh Castle Hill 108
Hartley 108
Hawarden Castle 38

136

INDEX

Hawes Bridge Castle 108
Hayes Castle 108
Hayton Castle 108
Henry I, king of England 36, 84
Henry II, king of England 17, 19, 36, 84, 107-8, 113-4
Henry IV, king of England 20
Henry VIII, king of England 30, 100
Herefordshire 2, 41, 83
Highhead Castle 108
Hollingworth 43
Holywell Castle 38
Hope valley 43
Hornby Castle 3, 8, 29, 108-9
Hosely Castle 38

I

Ireland 44
Irthington Castle 19, 109

K

Kendal Castle 109
Kent, river 17
King, Cathcart, castle historian 3, 9, 40, 109
Kirkby Lonsdale Castle 109
Kirkoswald Castle 109

L

Lancashire 2, 3, 5, 7, 10-1, 17, 19, 29-30, 38, 41, 51, 92, 94, 98, 102, 106, 108, 110, 112, 114
Lancaster Castle 2, 5, 10, 19, 19-20, 21, 29-30, 38, 102-3
Lathom House 5, 29-30
Liddel Castle 9, 14, 16
Liddel Strength 9, 14, 110
Liddel Water 14, 16
Lincoln 18-9, 37, 85
Liverpool Castle 3, 11, 103
London 18, 87

Tower of 47
Longdendale, Lordship of 1, 43-4, 83
Low Borrowbridge 18
Ludlow Castle 43
Lune, River & Valley 3, 8, 14, 17-8, 29

M

Macclesfield Castle 29, 40, 110
Malpas Castle 7, 8, 19, 20, 110
Manchester 3, 19
Manchester castle 5, 7, 110
university 57, 91, 95
See also Cheetham College
Maryport Castle 110
Melling Castle 14, 19, 104, 110
Mersey, river 12
Merseyside 5, 103, 111, 114
Micklehurst Brook 54
Millom Castle 110
Mold Castle 38
Monmouthshire 43
Morhull Castle 110
Mossley 92-3, 95
Mote Hill 3
Mottram 43, 87

N

Nantwich Castle 19, 110
Naworth castle 110-1
Newcastle-under-Lyme Castle 39
Newton-le-Willows Castle 111
Northumberland 22, 24-6, 28, 41
Northwich Castle 111
Norwich 18

O

Oldcastle 111
Ormerod, George, historian 91-3

P

Pendragon Castle 6, 10-11, 17, 111-2
Pennington Castle 112
Penrith Castle 9, 27-9, 104

Penwortham 3, 14, 19, 19, 111-2
Percival, Thomas, antiquarian 92, 91-3
Pevensey 19
Peveril Castle 34, 42-5, 46, 47-8, 53
Pickering Castle 54
Piel Castle 5, 26, 114-5
Prestatyn Castle 38
Preston Castle 3, 112
Pulford Castle 7, 14, 16, 38-9, 112

R

Radcliffe Tower 29
Raines, Canon Francis Robert, antiquarian 91, 94
Ranulf, sixth earl of Chester 11, 13, 19-20, 82-3
Restormel Castle 54
Ribble, river and valley 7, 17, 106, 112
Richard I, king of England 19, 37
Richard III, king of England 27
Robert the Bruce, king of Scotland 9, 29
Rochdale Castle 94, 112
Rochdale Castle 5, 7
Rose Castle 19, 115
Runcorn Castle 112

S

Saddleworth Geological Society 78, 91, 93
Salford, University of 57
Scaleby Castle 112
Scotland & Scots 2, 9, 14, 17, 28-9, 36, 81, 83, 99, 101-2, 105, 108, 110
Shap 14
Shipbrook Castle 112
Shocklack Oldcastle 112
Shotwick Castle 7, 14, 37, 104
Shrewsbury 38
Shropshire 38, 41, 43,

83
Skipton Castle 26
Staffordshire 38
Stanley Tower 29
Stayley 87-8
Stephen, king of England 33, 36, 81, 84, 116
Stockport Castle 7, 19, 29, 113
Stokesay Castle 22, 23
Surrey 54
Sussex 17, 24, 30

T

Tameside 43, 57, 85, 97
Tebay (Old) Castle 14, 113
Thurland Castle 30, 113
Tintwistle 43
Triermain Castle 114
Turner, Joseph, artist 3

U

Ullerwood Castle 7, 14, 39, 41, 107, 114

W

Wales 2, 7, 14-6, 21, 36-9, 41, 83, 101, 112
Warkworth Castle 25, 28
Warrington Castle 3, 114
Watch Hill Castle 5, 7, 14, 41, 113-4
Watson, Rev John 91-2
Westmorland 17, 39, 41-2
West Derby 5, 19, 114
Whittington Castle 19, 114
William I, King, 2, 19-8, 35
Windsor Castle 54
Wolsty Castle 115
Wrexham 38

Y

Yorkshire 10, 17, 26, 29, 53

137

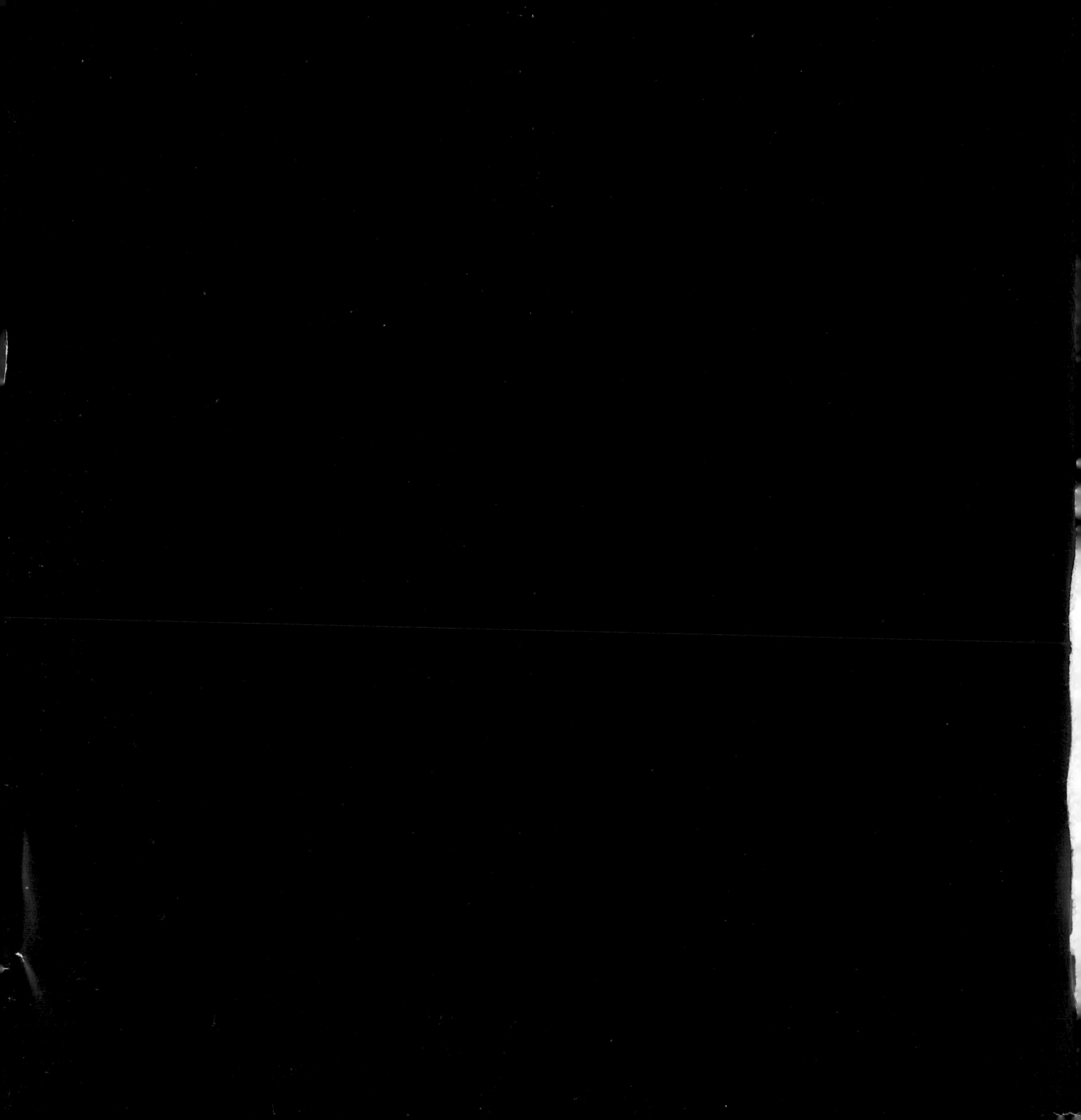